WHAT A YEAR IT WAS!

19 67

A walk back in time...

Happy Anniversary!

To *Chris & Sue*

From *Hilda & Gabe*

xo   40 Years - Wow!   xo

Dedicated to America's men and women
who risked and lost their lives
in the Vietnam War.

Publishers • Lawrence Siegel & Arthur Worthington
Designers • Peter Hess & Marguerite Jones
Writing & Research • Peter Hess & Debbie Sedley
Facilitator • Pamela Thomas
Series originated by Beverly Cohn

www.FLICKBACK.com
(800) 541-3533

Contents

Arts & Entertainment 5

In The News 57

   Politics and World Events 59

   People 75

   Human Interest 87

What's New 97

   New Products and Inventions 99

   Science 112

   Medicine 119

   It's a Living 129

Fashion 137

Sports 157

Arts & Entertainment

The man...and the motion picture that simply do not conform.

PAUL NEWMAN

COOL HAND LUKE

Paul Newman has a big year with the release of the western film *Hombre*, followed by his Best Actor Oscar®-nominated performance in *Cool Hand Luke*.

Movies

Big and small film studios alike exploit the new era of sexual liberation and relaxed moral standards to release movies which audiences find...

SHOCKING!

And, producers hope, irresistable. *Valley of the Dolls*—recounting Jacqueline Susann's sensational and sordid tale of avaricious career girls trapped in a consuming spiral of drugs, booze and sex—leads the pack. The notorious Swedish import *I Am Curious (Yellow)* ignites the *is-it-art?* or *is-it-porn?* debate nationwide, though few get around to actually seeing the film. Low-budget celluloid king Roger Corman contributes *The Trip* (psychedelia penned by Jack Nicholson and starring Peter Fonda) and *The St. Valentine's Day Massacre*. Playing at a drive-in near you are less illustrious entries in the sex, sleaze and violence parade, sporting titles which trumpet their attractions: *Devil's Angels*, *Weird World of LSD*, *Shanty Tramp*, *The Tiger and the Pussycat*, *Mondo Mod*, *The Hippie Revolt*, *Spree*, *Hot Rods to Hell*, *She Freak* and *The Girl, the Body, and the Pill.*

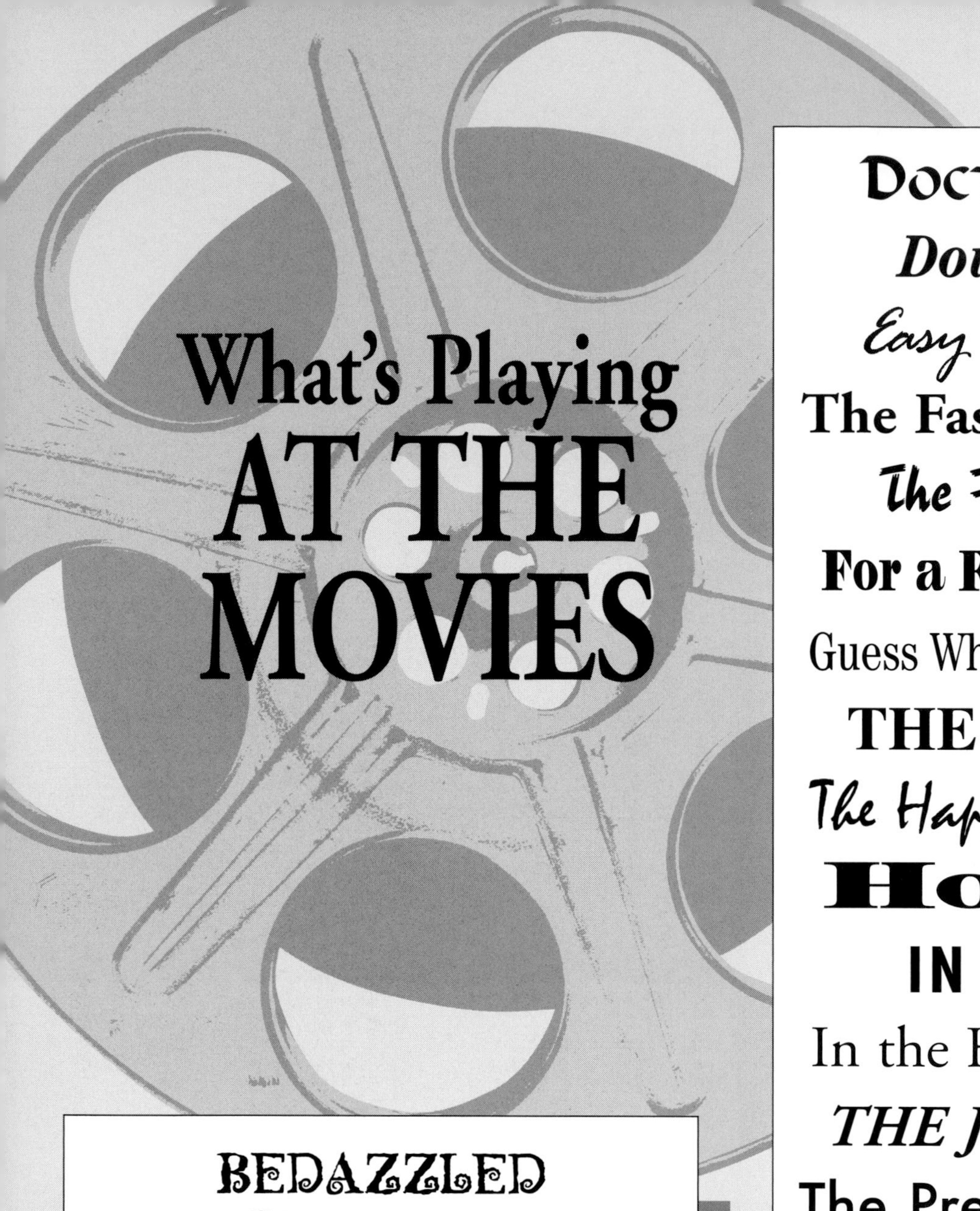

What's Playing AT THE MOVIES

DOCTOR DOLITTLE

Double Trouble

Easy Come, Easy Go

The Fastest Guitar Alive

The Flim-Flam Man

For a Few Dollars More

Guess Who's Coming to Dinner

THE GRADUATE

The Happiest Millionaire

Hombre

IN LIKE FLINT

In the Heat of the Night

THE JUNGLE BOOK

The President's Analyst

Reflections in a Golden Eye

SON OF GODZILLA

Tobruk

UP THE DOWN STAIRCASE

Wait Until Dark

The War Wagon

The Whisperers

BEDAZZLED

Belle de Jour

The Bobo

BONNIE and CLYDE

THE BORN LOSERS

CASINO ROYALE

Camelot

CLAMBAKE

Cool Hand Luke

THE STARS SHINE BRIGHTLY FOR 'MILLIE' PREMIERE

New York's Criterion Theater is the scene for the premiere of Universal's star-studded Technicolor musical, *Thoroughly Modern Millie.*

Singer Steve Lawrence arrives with wife Eydie Gormet.

Stars arrive on the red carpet in front of enthusiastic crowds. The gala event is a benefit for the Museum of the City of New York and one of Manhattan's major social events of the season.

At left is beautiful actress Lee Remick.

Actor Eli Wallach.

Ed Sullivan with Mrs. Sullivan.

Silver screen icon Myrna Loy.

First Lady of the American Theatre Ethel Merman is accompanied by composer Jimmy Van Heusen.

Van Heusen's songwriting partner Sammy Cahn arrives. They wrote "Millie's" original songs.

Carol Channing is one of the picture's co-stars.

Richard Chamberlain, TV's Dr. Kildare.

British actor James Fox is "Millie's" male lead, displaying his talent for comedy, song and dance.

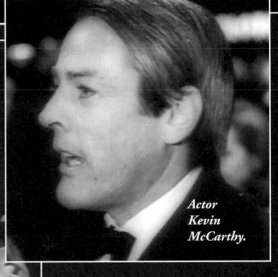

Actor Kevin McCarthy.

Mary Tyler Moore, at right, plays an orphan in the film—Miss Dorothy Brown.

Cast member Beatrice Lily is another First Lady of the stage.

Thoroughly Modern Millie stars Julie Andrews *(below)* and tunefully recalls the delightful days of the '20s .

11

The Academy Awards

"And The Winner Is..."

Oscars® Presented in 1967

BEST PICTURE
A MAN FOR ALL SEASONS

BEST ACTOR
PAUL SCOFIELD,
A Man For All Seasons

BEST ACTRESS
ELIZABETH TAYLOR,
Who's Afraid of Virginia Woolf?

BEST DIRECTOR
FRED ZINNEMANN,
A Man For All Seasons

BEST SUPPORTING ACTOR
WALTER MATTHAU, *The Fortune Cookie*

BEST SUPPORTING ACTRESS
SANDY DENNIS, *Who's Afraid of Virginia Woolf?*

BEST SONG
"BORN FREE," *Born Free*

Paul Scofield

1967 Favorites *(Oscars® Presented in 1968)*

BEST PICTURE
IN THE HEAT OF THE NIGHT

BEST ACTOR
ROD STEIGER,
In the Heat of the Night

BEST ACTRESS
KATHERINE HEPBURN,
Guess Who's Coming to Dinner

BEST DIRECTOR
MIKE NICHOLS,
The Graduate

BEST SUPPORTING ACTOR
GEORGE KENNEDY, *Cool Hand Luke*

BEST SUPPORTING ACTRESS
ESTELLE PARSONS, *Bonnie and Clyde*

BEST SONG
"TALK TO THE ANIMALS," *Doctor Dolittle*

Director Alfred Hitchcock receives the Academy's special Irving G. Thalberg Memorial Award

The 39th annual Academy Awards ceremony, hosted by **Bob Hope** at the Santa Monica Civic Auditorium on April 10, 1967, comes very close to being cancelled due to a labor strike. It settles only three hours before the broadcast.

Bob Hope circa 1960

For the first time in 25 years, sisters are nominated for best actress (**Lynn Redgrave** and **Vanessa Redgrave**).

All the major cast members of *Who's Afraid of Virginia Woolf?* are Oscar® nominated and **Richard Burton** and **Elizabeth Taylor** are the only married couple ever nominated in the same year. The film garners 13 nominations in all.

Elizabeth Taylor with her Oscar®.

NEW STARS of '67

Dustin **Hoffman**
Katherine **Ross**
Michael J. **Pollard**
Gene **Wilder**
Lesley Ann **Warren**

Dustin Hoffman

Katherine Ross

TOP GROSSING FILMS North America

1. *The Dirty Dozen*
2. *You Only Live Twice*
3. *Casino Royale*
4. *A Man For All Seasons*
5. *Thoroughly Modern Millie*
6. *Barefoot in the Park*
7. *To Sir, with Love*

D-Day began when the dirty dozen were done!

METRO GOLDWYN MAYER presents A KENNETH HYMAN PRODUCTION

The Dirty Dozen

GOLDEN GLOBE AWARDS

BEST PICTURE (Drama)
In the Heat of the Night

BEST PICTURE (Musical or Comedy)
The Graduate

ACTOR in a Leading Role (Drama)
Rod Steiger
In the Heat of the Night

ACTOR in a Leading Role (Musical or Comedy)
Richard Harris
Camelot

ACTRESS in a Leading Role (Drama)
Edith Evans
The Whisperers

ACTRESS in a Leading Role (Musical or Comedy)
Anne Bancroft
The Graduate

SUPPORTING ACTOR
Richard Attenborough
Doctor Dolittle

SUPPORTING ACTRESS
Carol Channing
Thoroughly Modern Millie

DIRECTOR
Mike Nichols
The Graduate

Sidney Poitier as teacher Mark Thackeray in To Sir, with Love.

Sidney Poitier enjoys a banner year with the release of a trio of racially-charged films in which he portrays an embattled teacher in *To Sir, with Love*, *In the Heat of the Night*'s police detective Virgil Tibbs, and the suitor meeting his prospective in-laws in *Guess Who's Coming to Dinner*.

Steiger

While filming *Heat*, director **Norman Jewison** asks **Rod Steiger** to consider chewing gum throughout his Oscar®-winning role as the bigoted small-town Mississippi sheriff. Resistant at first, Steiger warms to the idea and chews his way through 263 packs of gum.

In addition to Steiger's Best Actor award, *In the Heat of the Night* scores four Oscars®, including Best Picture, Best Film Editing, Best Sound, and Best Writing.

Guess Who's Coming to Dinner enables **Katharine Hepburn** to earn her tenth nomination and second Oscar® for her portrayal of Christina Drayton, whose daughter is considering interracial marriage. Hepburn's niece, **Katharine Houghton**, appears as Drayton's daughter. Co-star **Spencer Tracy** dies 17 days after filming completes, and Hepburn never sees the finished movie, saying the memories of long-time love Tracy are too painful.

Hepburn

Robert Redford initially tests for the part of *The Graduate*'s Benjamin Braddock, but director **Mike Nichols** isn't convinced he can persuasively portray the underdog. "Let's put it this way," Nichols reputedly says to Redford. "Have you ever struck out with a girl?" "What do you mean?" Redford asks. "That's precisely my point," replies Nichols. **Charles Grodin** *does* get the part, but that deal falls apart because of a salary dispute. Finally, **Dustin Hoffman** winds up as Benjamin.

Robert Redford

Anne Bancroft's Mrs. Robinson character is supposed to be much older than Benjamin, but in reality, Bancroft and Dustin Hoffman are only about six years apart in age.

While shooting *The Graduate*'s hotel room encounter, Anne Bancroft is unaware that Hoffman is required to grab her breast. When he does, director Mike Nichols begins laughing loudly off-screen, causing Hoffman to break into laughter as well. Hoffman turns away from the camera and bangs his head on the wall in an effort to control himself. The scene is so funny, Nichols decides to leave it in.

The Graduate eventually grosses over $100 million, and the American Film Institute will rank it as the 7th best American film of the 20th century.

Anne Bancroft and Dustin Hoffman in a scene from The Graduate.

Show-a-rama, sponsored by the United Motion Picture Association, singles out **DON KNOTTS** with the Family Favorite Award for his performance in Universal's *The Reluctant Astronaut*. Knotts, popular with the public and the motion picture exhibitors alike, is saluted by the assembled showmen.

Memorable Lines

Peter Sellers
David Niven
Woody Allen

CASINO ROYALE

Jimmy Bond: *You can't shoot me! I have a very low threshold of death. My doctor says I can't have bullets enter my body at any time.*

The Detainer: *You're crazy. You are absolutely crazy!*
Jimmy Bond: *People called Einstein crazy.*
The Detainer: *That's not true. No one ever called Einstein crazy.*
Jimmy Bond: *Well, they would have if he'd carried on like this.*

COOL HAND LUKE

Boss Paul: *That ditch is Boss Kean's ditch. And I told him that dirt in it's your dirt. What's your dirt doin' in his ditch?*
Luke: *I don't know, Boss.*
Boss Paul: *You better get in there and get it out, boy.*

Paul Newman

Captain: *What we've got here is... failure to communicate.*

l to r Gene Hackman, Estelle Parsons, Warren Beatty, Faye Dunaway, Michael J. Pollard

Bonnie and Clyde

Clyde Barrow: *This here's Miss Bonnie Parker. I'm Clyde Barrow. We rob banks.*

Clyde Barrow: *Don't you believe what you read in all them newspapers. That's the law talkin' there. They want us to look big so they gonna look big when they catch us. And they ain't gonna catch us. 'Cause I'm even better at runnin' than I am at robbin' banks!*

Camelot

Richard Harris

King Arthur: *Merlin told me once, "Never be too disturbed if you don't understand what a woman is thinking. They don't do it very often."*

King Arthur (to Mordred): *Far more seasoned rascals than you have polished their souls. I advise you, get out the wax. Better to be rubbed clean than rubbed out.*

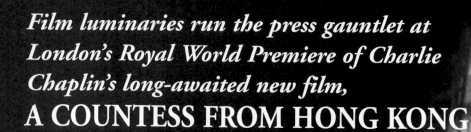

Film luminaries run the press gauntlet at London's Royal World Premiere of Charlie Chaplin's long-awaited new film,

A COUNTESS FROM HONG KONG

Chaplin wrote, directed and composed the music for the film. Sophia Loren stars, along with Marlon Brando, who flies in from Hollywood for the event. Eight members of the Chaplin family attend as well.

Douglas Fairbanks is among the first night celebrities.

The Maestro, Charlie Chaplin

Chaplin family members

Liza Minelli

Tippi Hedren is in the movie.

Marlon Brando, attracting lots of attention.

Princess Alexandra, cousin of the Queen, receives a bouqet.

BORN IN 1967 ★
PAMELA ANDERSON
OLIVIA D'ABO ★ TIA
CARRERE ★ LAURA
DERN ★ WILL FERRELL
JAMIE FOXX ★ NICOLE KIDMAN
JULIA ROBERTS ★ LIEV
SCHREIBER ★ ANNA
NICOLE SMITH
BENICIO DEL TORO
EMILY WATSON ★

Nicole Kidman

Benicio del Toro

James Bond fans have a lot to smile about with the all-star spoof *Casino Royale* finding retired agent 007 **David Niven** coping with a number of ersatz Bonds, played by—among others—**Woody Allen** and **Peter Sellers**. Meanwhile, the suave spy travels to Tokyo and outer space in *You Only Live Twice*, which insists that **Sean Connery** *IS* James Bond!

Elvis Presley-lovers see double with the release of 2 of his flicks. *Double Trouble* has Elvis in swingin' London tracking jewel thieves, while he's a Florida 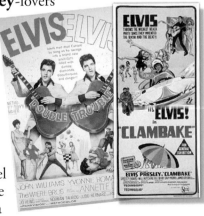 water ski instructor in *Clambake*, where the sun shines, the songs flow and the girls abound.

Hollywood Bids a Fond Farewell

BERT LAHR (72), best known for his role as the Cowardly Lion in *The Wizard of Oz*, dies of cancer.

British Actress **VIVIEN LEIGH** (46) succumbs to tuberculosis, which she suffered chronically. She achieved success on the stage, but gained her greatest fame in films, twice winning the Best Actress Oscar® for her performances as Scarlett O'Hara in *Gone With The Wind* (1939) and as Blanche DuBois in *A Streetcar Named Desire*. Former husband, actor Laurence Olivier, was a frequent collaborator in the theatre; they divorced in 1960.

Spencer Tracy

Platinum blond actress and sex symbol **JAYNE MANSFIELD** (34) is killed in an auto accident.

Labeled "The Oomph Girl," actress **ANN SHERIDAN** (52) dies of cancer. She had success in many films throughout the 30s and 40s, including *Angels With Dirty Faces*, *They Drive by Night* and *Kings Row*.

Acclaimed actor **SPENCER TRACY** dies of heart failure at age 67, less than three weeks after finishing his last film, *Guess Who's Coming to Dinner*. Tracy won back-to-back Best Actor Oscars® for *Captains Courageous* (1937) and *Boys Town* (1938). Additionally, he received nominations for his work in 7 other films, including *Father of the Bride* (1950), *Bad Day at Black Rock* (1955), *The Old Man and the Sea* (1958) and *Inherit the Wind* (1960). In 1941, he began a relationship with Katharine Hepburn, with whom he teamed in a number of popular films.

Vivien Leigh

Introducing...Color TV with a picture so easy to tune you can do it blindfolded!

Why not get the best

Zenith's Automatic Fine-tuning Control tunes color television picture-perfect at the flick of a finger! Just flip the switch once and forget it . . . because it not only *tunes* the color picture . . . but *keeps* it tuned as you change from channel to channel. And it even perfects your fine-tuning on UHF channels . . . automatically.

How does it work? Instantly, electronically, it seeks out and locks in the perfect color picture signal to bring you Color TV's sharpest picture.

Zenith's exclusive Sunshine® Color Picture Tube has a new rare earth phosphor for greater picture brightness with more true-to-life color.

And you'll be enjoying Color TV's largest rectangular picture . . . 295 square inches of brilliant color.

You'll also be enjoying famous Zenith Handcrafted quality throughout. Every Zenith Color Chassis is carefully handwired for unrivaled dependability. There are no printed circuits. No production shortcuts.

See Zenith's Automatic Fine-tuning Control on a wide selection of fine furniture consoles at your Zenith dealer's now.

Featured at left, the Andalucia Model X4543DE in beautiful Mediterranean styling.

The Handcrafted Color TV

ZENITH®
The quality goes in before the name goes on

18

Television

CAROL BURNETT: *In For The Long Haul*

In September, when CBS launches a new comedy variety series called *The Carol Burnett Show*, few realize that they are witnessing the birth of a television institution; however, the lithe comedienne with the rubber face makes an immediate connection with her audience and the show becomes a small screen fixture for the next eleven years, along the way scooping up 25 Emmys and 8 Golden Globes. Abetted by a who's-who roster of guest stars and an ensemble of talented regulars—**Harvey Korman**, **Vicki Lawrence**, **Lyle Waggoner** and later, **Tim Conway**—Burnett romps weekly through endearing dances and songs and riotous comedy sketches which have the crowd, and frequently the performers, in stitches.

One of Carol Burnett's recurring characters, the charwoman.

Dick (top) and Tom sandwich guest Inger Stevens.

MOM ALWAYS LIKED YOU BEST

CBS scores another surprise hit in the comedy-variety stakes with *The Smothers Brothers Comedy Hour*. Originally scheduled as a mid-season replacement going up against NBC's seemingly indomitable *Bonanza*, the Smothers follow in the wake of the successive failures of a number of venerable entries—but the combative banter and folk songs of siblings Tom and Dick have an irreverent appeal and they catch on—maybe not so surprising considering their string of hit comedy albums and a youthful following.

19

NEW on TV

Ironside

Raymond Burr (center) is wheelchair-bound ex-cop Robert T. Ironside, aided by (l-r) Don Galloway, Elizabeth Baur, Don Mitchell.

Sally Field is Sister Bertrille,
The Flying Nun.

Mannix
stars Mike Connors as private eye Joe Mannix.

Say Goodbye to...

Gilligan's Island
What's My Line
The Milton Berle Show
Juke Box Jury

MORE PREMIERES **Maya** *with Jay North* • **Gentle Ben** *with Clint Howard, Dennis Weaver*
The **Phil Donahue Show** debuts in Dayton, Ohio

PRIMETIME LINEUP

		7:00	7:30	8:00	8:30	9:00	9:30	10:00	10:30
SATURDAY	ABC	Local	The Dating Game	The Newlywed Game	Lawrence Welk Show		Iron Horse		ABC Scope
	CBS	Local	Jackie Gleason Show		My Three Sons	Hogan's Heroes	Petticoat Junction	Mannix	
	NBC	Local	Maya		Get Smart	Saturday Night at the Movies			
SUNDAY	ABC	Voyage to the Bottom of the Sea		The FBI		The ABC Sunday Night Movie			
	CBS	Local	Gentle Ben	Ed Sullivan Show		Smothers Brothers Comedy Hour		Mission: Impossible	
	NBC	Local	Walt Disney's Wonderful World of Color		Mothers-in-Law	Bonanza		The High Chaparral	
MONDAY	ABC	Local	Cowboy in Africa		The Rat Patrol	The Felony Squad	Peyton Place	The Big Valley	
	CBS	Local	Gunsmoke		The Lucy Show	Andy Griffith Show	Family Affair	Carol Burnett Show	
	NBC	Local	The Monkees	The Man from U.N.C.L.E.		Danny Thomas Hour		I Spy	
TUESDAY	ABC	Local	Garrison's Gorillas		The Invaders		N.Y.P.D.	The Hollywood Palace	
	CBS	Local	Daktari		Red Skelton Hour		Good Morning World	CBS News Hour	
	NBC	Local	I Dream of Jeannie	Jerry Lewis Show		Tuesday Night at the Movies			
WEDNESDAY	ABC	Local	Custer		Second 100 Years	The ABC Wednesday Night Movie and Specials			
	CBS	Local	Lost in Space		The Beverly Hillbillies	Green Acres	He & She	Dundee and the Culhane	
	NBC	Local	The Virginian			The Kraft Music Hall		Run for Your Life	
THURSDAY	ABC	Local	Batman	The Flying Nun	Bewitched	That Girl	Peyton Place	Good Company	Local
	CBS	Local	Cimarron Strip			The CBS Thursday Night Movies			
	NBC	Local	Daniel Boone		Ironside		Dragnet 1968	Dean Martin Show	
FRIDAY	ABC	Local	Off to See the Wizard		Hondo			Judd, for the Defense	
	CBS	Local	The Wild, Wild West		Gomer Pyle, USMC	The CBS Friday Night Movies			
	NBC	Local	Tarzan		Star Trek		Accidental Family	NBC News Specials/ Bell Telephone Hour	

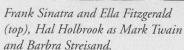

Frank Sinatra and Ella Fitzgerald (top), Hal Holbrook as Mark Twain and Barbra Streisand.

IMPORTS

A number of programs from across the pond brighten American television screens. The UK exports the children's program, *Do Not Adjust Your Set* featuring future members of Monty Python's Flying Circus **Eric Idle**, **Terry Jones** and **Michael Palin**. Also from England comes *The Prisoner* which stars **Patrick McGoohan** as a secret agent held captive in a resort town. The unusual series still enjoys a cult following. *The Forsyte Saga*, a period BBC dramatic series, is hugely popular with American audiences and is the first British television program ever to be sold to the USSR. And, from Canada comes the children's program *Mr. Dressup*.

The TV Special comes of age, with NBC airing 15 primetime specials in the first two weeks of December alone.

Among the more outstanding offerings: *Frank Sinatra: A Man and his Music + Ella + Jobim* featuring Ol' Blue Eyes with jazz singer Fitzgerald and Brazilian composer Antonio Carlos Jobim; a three-part report on the Warren Commission's investigation of the JFK assasination; Hallmark Hall of Fame's *St. Joan*; Hal Holbrook's one-man show *Mark Twain Tonight*; and Barbra Streisand's *The Belle of 14th Street*, which presents the singer with guest stars in a vaudeville theme.

Patrick McGoohan, The Prisoner

The Beatles captivate television audiences worldwide, debuting their video for *Hello, Goodbye* on the ED SULLIVAN SHOW, appearing on AMERICAN BANDSTAND with performances of *Strawberry Fields Forever* and *Penny Lane*, and playing *All You Need Is Love* for 400 million people in 30 countries on ONE WORLD, the first live international television broadcast via satellite. In addition, their *Magical Mystery Tour* film is broadcast for the first time on British TV.

Chris Rock

NEIGHBORHOOD TROLLEY

Children's favorite *Mr. Roger's Neighborhood* premieres.

CBS announces plans to cancel mainstay **Gunsmoke** but protests from as high up as the U.S. Congress bring a reprieve and a move from Saturday to Monday evening.

IN LIVING COLOR

With sales of color TV sets on the rise and 23% of U.S. households owning color sets by year's end, all CBS soaps abandon black and white and most television broadcasts are in color.

The BBC2 becomes Europe's first color TV broadcaster with its live coverage from the Wimbledon Tennis Championships, and color TV broadcasts begin in the Philippines.

1966 - 1967 EMMY awards

Best Drama Series
Mission: Impossible

Best Actor in a Drama Series
Bill Cosby
I Spy

Best Actress in a Drama Series
Barbara Bain
Mission: Impossible

Best Supporting Actor in a Drama Series
Milburn Stone
Gunsmoke

Best Supporting Actress in a Drama Series
Barbara Anderson
Ironside

Best Comedy Series
Get Smart

Best Actor in a Comedy Series
Don Adams
Get Smart

Best Actress in a Comedy Series
Lucille Ball
The Lucy Show

Best Supporting Actor in a Comedy Series
Werner Klemperer
Hogan's Heroes

Best Supporting Actress in a Comedy Series
Marion Lorne
Bewitched

The Corporation for Public Broadcasting (CPB) is established and PBS begins as a 70-station network.

1967 ADVERTISEMENT

MOTOROLA
RECTANGULAR
COLOR TV
in magnificent cabinets by Drexel
American Review Styling
Model CD888D
Built-in casters. Genuine Maple Veneers and Maple Solids with Drexel American Review Vintage Cherry finish. 30¾" high, 35" wide, 19" deep.*
Cordillera Styling
Model CD887D
Built-in casters. Genuine Pecan Veneers and Pecan Solids with Drexel Cordillera finish. 30" high, 35⅝" wide, 19⅛" deep.*
Declaration Styling
Model CD886D
Built-in casters. Genuine Walnut Veneers and Walnut Solids with Drexel Declaration Walnut finish. 29⅝" high, 32" wide, 17⅛" deep.*
MOTOROLA
23" RECTANGULAR CONSOLE
COLOR TV
23" picture measured diagonally; 295 sq. in.
WITH SOLID STATE COMPONENTS AT 17 VITAL POINTS FOR SPACE AGE RELIABILITY
All 82 Channel UHF/VHF
Contemporary Styling
Model CL883D
Golden Voice 5" speaker. Genuine Walnut Veneers and Select Hardwood Solids with Oil Walnut finish. 28¾" high, 35⅝" wide, 20⅝" deep.*
Early American Styling
Model CL885D
Golden Voice 5" speaker. Genuine Oak Veneers and Oak Solids with Country Oak finish. 30⅞" high, 34¼" wide, 18¾" deep.*
Mediterranean Styling
Model CL884D
Golden Voice 5" speaker. Genuine Oak Veneers and Oak Solids with Burnished Oak finish. 30¼" high, 34⅝" wide, 18½" deep.*
Mediterranean Styling
Model CU837D
Select Hardwood Veneers and Solids with an applied North American Pecan grain finish. 29⅝" high, 32⅜" wide, 18¼" deep.*
Early American Styling
Model CU836D
Genuine Birch Veneers and Select Hardwood Soli
Brushed Glaze Maple finish. 31½" high, 32⅜" wi
18¾" deep.*
Contemporary Styling
Model CL882D
Golden Voice 5" speaker. Genuine Walnut Veneers and Select Hardwood Solids with Light Oil Walnut finish. 29¾" high, 34⅝" wide, 18⅝" deep.*
French Provincial Styling
Model CU838D
Genuine Gum Pocket Cherry Veneers and Select Hardwood Solids with Gum Pocket Cherry finish. 29⅝" high, 32⅜" wide, 18¼" deep.*
Contemporary Styling
Model CU835D
Genuine Tiama Mahogany Veneers and Select Hardwood Solids with Traditional Mahogany finish or Genuine Walnut Veneers and Select Hardwood Solids with Oil Walnut finish. 29½" high, 32⅜" wide, 18¼" deep.*
Contemporary Styling
Model CU805D
Select Hardwood Veneers and Solids with an app
Walnut grain finish. 31½" high, 30¾" wide, 17¾"
MOTOROLA
23" RECTANGULAR TABLE
COLOR TV
23" picture measured diagonally; 295 sq. in.
BIGGEST PICTURE
IN TABLE COLOR TV
Model CT802D
Golden Voice 4" x 6" speaker. Durable Metal Cabinet in Dark Metallic Brown color. 19¾" high, 28⅝" wide, 21¾" deep. (Depth includes tube cap.)

Radio

A *Variety* poll reports that over 95 percent of all people above 11 years of age listen to radio programs during the course of a week. As AM and FM programming grows more diverse, the *New York Times Magazine* describes 1967 as "radio's fractionalization" period. Many stations switch to new formats—all-talk, all-news, all-pop, all-jazz, etc. ABC Radio announces plans to provide affiliates with a choice of four different radio feeds, each with a different format: American-contemporary, FM, Personality-Entertainment, and Information.

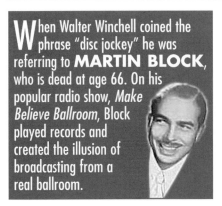

When Walter Winchell coined the phrase "disc jockey" he was referring to **MARTIN BLOCK**, who is dead at age 66. On his popular radio show, *Make Believe Ballroom*, Block played records and created the illusion of broadcasting from a real ballroom.

Art Linkletter's CBS radio show, *House Party*, is cancelled, ending a 23-year run.

The Public Broadcasting Act of 1967 leads to the start of National Public Radio in the United States.

BBC and BEYOND

BBC Radio Leicester is Britain's first local radio station, and Radio 1 becomes the first national pop station.

University Radio York is Britain's first student radio station, and the country's first independent station.

The British Marine Broadcasting Offenses Act passes, making it an offense to advertise or supply an offshore radio station from the UK. All of Britain's offshore pirate radio stations close, except Radio Caroline, which originally began transmission from a ship anchored off the coast of South East England in International waters.

Southern Asia's Radio Ceylon becomes the Ceylon Broadcasting Corporation.

3AW is Australia's first talk radio station.

KHJ Radio Los Angeles "Boss 30" Records May 10, 1967

1	Groovin'	Young Rascals
2	Respect	Aretha Franklin
3	Somebody To Love	Jefferson Airplane
4	Dry Your Eyes	Brenda & The Tabulations
5	The Happening	Supremes
6	The Flower Children	Marcia Strassman
7	I Think We're Alone Now	Tommy James & The Shondells
8	I Got Rhythm	Happenings
9	Six O'Clock	Lovin' Spoonful
10	Sweet Soul Music	Arthur Conley
11	When I Was Young	Eric Burdon & The Animals
12	Blue's Theme	Davie Allan & The Arrows
13	Sunshine Girl	Parade
14	She'd Rather Be With Me	Turtles
15	Creeque Alley	Mamas & Papas
16	Can't Seem to Make You Mine	Seeds
17	Him Or Me - What's It Gonna Be	Paul Revere & The Raiders
18	Society's Child	Janis Ian
19	Friday On My Mind	Easybeats
20	Girl, You'll Be A Woman Soon	Neil Diamond
21	Let's Live For Today	Grass Roots
22	All I Need	Temptations
23	Don't You Care	Buckinghams
24	Windy	Association
25	I Was Kaiser Bill's Batman	Whistling Jack Smith
26	On A Carousel	Hollies
27	Shake A Tail Feather	James & Bobby Purify
28	Light My Fire	Doors
29	I'll Make Him Love Me	Barbara Lewis
30	You Got What It Takes	Dave Clark Five

BILL GRAHAM PRESENTS IN SAN FRANCISCO

5 DAYS OF SOUND
DEC. 26 - NEW YEARS EVE
THE DOORS
CHUCK BERRY
SALVATION
DEC. 26 · 27 · 28
LIGHTS BY HOLY SEE

DEC. 29 - 30
CHUCK BERRY
BIG BROTHER
AND THE HOLDING CO.
QUICKSILVER
MESSENGER SERVICE
LIGHTS BY GLENN McKAY'S HEADLIGHTS
THE FILLMORE SCENE
AT WINTERLAND
PLUS NEW YEARS - JEFFERSON AIRPLANE
BIG BROTHER AND THE HOLDING CO. ·
MESSENGER SERVICE and FREEDOM

NEW HAMPSHIRE COLLEGE
PRESENTS
MITCH RYDER
AND REVUE

FRIDAY, APRIL 28. 1967

The Blues Mago
Are going on a Chartered Flying Tour to these

FRIDAY, JAN. 20	NYC to Boston, Mass. (entire day)	FRIDAY, JAN. 27	St. Louis (all day
SATURDAY, JAN. 21	Boston to Baltimore–Washington DC area	SATURDAY, JAN. 28	To De Moines (travel to St. Pa
SUNDAY, JAN. 22	Baltimore-Washington area	SUNDAY, JAN. 29	St. Paul/Minnea (2-4 j.m. show)
MONDAY, JAN. 23	To Pittsburgh, Pa. (overnight)	MONDAY, JAN. 30	To Milwaukee (overnight)
TUESDAY, JAN. 24	To Columbus, Ohio stops only) On to Dayton, Ohio (overnight)	TUESDAY, JAN. 31	To Toledo (all da
WEDNESDAY, JAN. 25	To Cincinnati, Ohio (overnight)	WEDNESDAY, FEB. 1	To Erie—Buffalo
THURSDAY, JAN. 26	To Louisville, Ky. (stops) On to St. Louis, Mo. (overnight)	THURSDAY, FEB. 2	To Syracuse-Roc (overnight)
		FRIDAY, FEB. 2	To Hartford

PSYCHEDELIC LOLLIPOP
BLUES MAGOOS

Hit single from the alb

NEW FROM THE *Mothers* of Invention
WE'RE ONLY IN IT FOR THE MONEY

BRIAN EPSTEIN/NEMS PRESENTS
CREAM
SUN JULY 2
SAVILLE THEATRE
SHAFTESBURY AVE LONDON

BLUE NOTE
THE **JAZZ SOUND** FOR EVERYONE

FREAK OUT! & ABSOLUTELY FREEEEE
THRILLING CLEAN FUN!
NOW!

PICKED BY BILLBOARD, CASH BOX, RECORD WORLD ..and jumping up the charts...

Buffalo Springfield

"FOR WHAT IT'S WORTH"
(STOP, HEY WHAT'S THAT SOUND)
ATCO 6459

WAKE UP TO
"INCENSE AND PEPPERMINTS" BY THE STRAWBERRY ALARM CLOCK

THE ALBUM INCLUDES THE HIT SINGLE.
STEREO 73014   MONO 3014
© UNIVERSAL CITY RECORDS · A Division of MCA Inc.

26

Popular Music

Nearly a quarter million music fans mass across three days in Monterey, California for the historic **MONTEREY INTERNATIONAL POP FESTIVAL** where they bask in the glow of over 30 assembled rock, pop, folk and r&b acts. The original event of its kind, with most of the performers donating their time for charity, it casts the mold for all future rock festivals, though few are able to quite capture the magic generated by the summit gathering of the "Summer of Love."

Blissful attendees witness the first eagerly-anticipated major American appearances by guitar god **Jimi Hendrix** and Britain's **The Who**, and the exposure catapults singer **Janis Joplin** (who performs twice) and soul shouter **Otis Redding** from rumored phenomenons to headliners. A number of future rock mainstays emerge from Monterey with recording contracts. Notable for their absence are the **Beatles** (who no longer perform live, though **Paul McCartney** sits on the festival board), the **Rolling Stones** (**Brian Jones**, who attends, is dubbed "King of the Festival") and **Bob Dylan**. Though they are among the event's organizers, the **Beach Boys** cancel at the last minute.

The Who

Ravi Shankar

Canned Heat

The Byrds

Jefferson Airplane

The Mamas and The Papas

THE PERFORMERS

FRI JUNE 16
The Association
The Paupers
Lou Rawls
Beverly
Johnny Rivers
The Animals
Simon and
    Garfunkel

SAT JUNE 17
Canned Heat
Big Brother &
    The Holding Co.
    w/ Janis Joplin
Country Joe and
    The Fish
Al Kooper
The Butterfield
    Blues Band

Quicksilver
    Messenger Service
Steve Miller Band
The Electric Flag
Moby Grape
Hugh Masekela
The Byrds
Laura Nyro
Jefferson Airplane
Booker T &
    The MG's
Otis Redding

SUN JUNE 18
Ravi Shankar
The Blues Project
Big Brother &
    The Holding Co.
    w/ Janis Joplin
The Group With
    No Name
Buffalo Springfield
The Who
Grateful Dead
The Jimi Hendrix
    Experience
Scott McKenzie
The Mamas &
    The Papas

Otis Redding

Janis Joplin

The Jimi Hendrix Experience

27

*A*longside the Monterey Pop Festival, the unveiling of the **Beatles'** album *Sgt. Pepper's Lonely Hearts Club Band* ranks among the signature events of the 60s. Certified "gold" the same day as its June release, it tops charts worldwide, holding the number one slot in Britain for 27 weeks and 19 weeks in America, and proves an immediate popular and critical success. Its innovative production, adventurous instrumentation and arrangement, sly lyrical references and, chiefly, its tuneful songs make it possibly the most influential rock album ever recorded.

The striking cover design by British pop art pioneer **Peter Blake** depicts the Beatles alongside cut-outs and wax figures from Madame Tussaud's museum, representing over 70 artists, actors and individuals the Beatles like or who influenced them in one way or another.

WHAT'S IN A NAME?
Some Colorful New Band Names

Electric Prunes

Strawberry Alarm Clock

Peanut Butter Conspiracy

Quicksilver Messenger Service

Blue Cheer

Procol Harum

Moody Blues

Flamin' Groovies

Vanilla Fudge

Electric Flag

Moby Grape

Blue Oyster Cult

Velvet Underground

Blues Magoos

Exploding, Inevitably

*T*he influence of hallucinogenic drugs such as LSD and mescaline on popular culture in general and pop music in particular becomes apparent to the nation during 1967s "Summer of Love." While an Austin band is the first to formally link the psychedelia label with music via their album titled *The Psychedelic Sounds of **the 13th Floor Elevators***, San Francisco bands are already heeding the dictum of drug guru **Timothy Leary** to "Turn On, Tune In, Drop Out." The long guitar solos and electronic distortions employed by bands like the **Grateful Dead** and **Jefferson Airplane** make the notion of the three-minute record track designed for radio airplay seem quaint. Songs like Jefferson Airplane's *White Rabbit*, *Purple Haze* by **Jimi Hendrix** and **Donovan**'s *Sunshine Superman* are among the many rife with drug references and imagery, and with the release of the **Beatles'** *Sgt. Pepper*, the counterculture truly explodes onto the international consciousness.

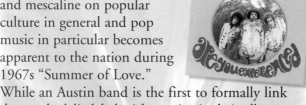

LPs by Hendrix, Donovan and the Grateful Dead

Breaking the Sound Barrier

By the time of **The Who**'s American debut, the group already has a reputation dating back to their hardscrabble club days for destroying instruments. Nearing the conclusion of *My Generation* at the Monterey Pop Festival, they up the ante when guitarist **Pete Townshend** sends up a fireball by jamming his guitar into a speaker while **Keith Moon** demolishes his drum kit with pre-planted explosives. Not to be outdone, **Jimi Hendrix** feigns copulation with a big amplifier during his Monterey *Wild Thing* finale, and "sacrifices" his guitar by first setting it on fire with lighter fluid, then smashing it to bits before a rapt crowd.

CHART BUSTERS

I'm a Believer ...The Monkees
Tell It Like It Is ...Aaron Neville
Sugar Town .....Nancy Sinatra
That's Life ......Frank Sinatra
Words of Love ...The Mamas & Papas
Standing in the
Shadows of Love ..The Four Tops
Mellow Yellow ..Donovan
Georgy Girl .....The Seekers
Kind of a Drag ...The Buckinghams
The Beat Goes On .Sonny and Cher
Gimme Some Lovin' Spencer Davis Group
Penny Lane ....The Beatles
Happy Together ..The Turtles
There's a Kind
of Hush ....Herman's Hermits
Bernadette .....The Four Tops
Strawberry
Fields Forever ...The Beatles
Something Stupid .Frank & Nancy Sinatra
I Think We're
Alone, Now .....Tommy James & Shondells
I Never Loved a Man the Way
I Love You ......Aretha Franklin
Jimmy Mack ....Martha & the Vandellas
Sweet Soul Music .Arthur Conley
The Happening ..The Supremes
Close Your Eyes .Peaches and Herb
Respect ....Aretha Franklin
Release Me .....Englebert Humperdinck
Girl, You'll Be a
Woman Soon ...Neil Diamond
Somebody to Love Jefferson Airplane
All I Need Is You .The Temptations
Windy ....The Association
Can't Take My Eyes
Off of You ......Frankie Valli
Live For Today ...The Grass Roots
Don't Sleep In
The Subway ....Petula Clark
Up, Up and Away The Fifth Dimension
Light My Fire ....The Doors
C'mon Marianne .The Four Seasons
A Whiter Shade
Of Pale ....Procol Harum
I Was Made To
Love Her ....Stevie Wonder
All You Need
Is Love ....The Beatles
Pleasant Valley
Sunday ....The Monkees
Carrie Anne .....The Hollies
Ode to Billy Joe .Bobbie Gentry
Reflections .....Diana Ross & Supremes
You're My Everything .The Temptations
The Letter .....Box Tops
Funky Broadway .Wilson Pickett
Never My Love ..The Association
Higher and Higher Jackie Wilson
Brown Eyed Girl .Van Morrison
Gimme Little Sign .Brenton Wood
To Sir, with Love .Lulu
Soul Man ....Sam and Dave
It Must Be Him ..Vikki Carr
Hello Goodbye ...The Beatles
Chain of Fools ...Aretha Franklin
Bend Me,
Shape Me .....The American Breed

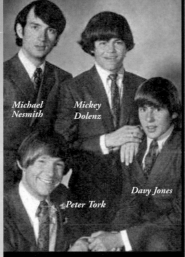

THE MONKEES are the top-selling group of the year, scoring hits with I'm a Believer, Daydream Believer, and Pleasant Valley Sunday.

Michael Nesmith   Mickey Dolenz
Peter Tork   Davy Jones

54-46 That's My Number by **Toots & the Maytals** is one of the first popular reggae songs; **Neil Diamond**'s *Red, Red Wine* is the first pop-reggae hit.

•

Frank Zappa's *Absolutely Free* is the first rock opera.

•

The Doors break through with their eponymous debut LP which includes *Light My Fire*.

•

The British rock group **Traffic** forms • **Pink Floyd** releases their first LP, *The Piper at the Gates of Dawn* • **Donny Hathaway**, **Ted Nugent**, **George Clinton**, **Sly and the Family Stone** and **Iggy Pop** are among new artists making a mark.

Sonny & Cher's* The Beat Goes On *is a hit.

SOME IMPORTANT ALBUMS

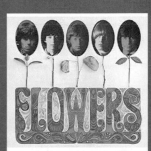

British blues-rock power trio **Cream** (**Eric Clapton**, **Jack Bruce** and **Ginger Baker**) follow up their debut collection *Fresh Cream* with the psychedelic *Disraeli Gears*. Reaching the top five on both the UK and US charts, it includes the smash hit *Sunshine of Your Love.*

Three **Rolling Stones** albums are released in 1967. *Between the Buttons* and the singles/miscellaneous collection *Flowers* contain monster hits including *Ruby Tuesday, Let's Spend The Night Together, Lady Jane* and *She's A Rainbow.* A third LP, *Their Satanic Majesties Request,* is the Stones' entry into the psychedelia derby and is generally regarded as less than an overwhelming success despite its groovy 3-D cover.

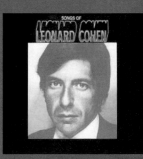

Bob Dylan continues to go his own way. *John Wesley Harding,* his first new work following the much publicized motorcycle accident of '66, is a simultaneously bright and brooding, visionary return to acoustic instrumentation. Also seeing release is *Bob Dylan's Greatest Hits,* his first compilation.

Songs of **Leonard Cohen** is the Canadian singer-songwriter's debut recording, though he is already regarded as a significant poet and novelist. Bitter, biting, funny and boasting the hit *Suzanne,* it is the opening salvo of an enduring and influential artist.

Distinctive, difficult to pigeon-hole song-stylist/pianist **Nina Simone** offers her loyal fans 3 LPs: *Silk and Soul; Nina Simone Sings the Blues* and *High Priestess of Soul.* Some of her most affecting renderings are here, including *Brown-Eyed Handsome Man* and *The House of the Rising Sun.*

Dionne Warwick

Aretha Franklin

Silk & Sass

Two women who dominate 1967's pop charts provide a study in contrasts. The picture of sophistication, singer DIONNE WARWICK's supple voice and witty delivery furnish song-writers Burt Bacharach and Hal David with the perfect vehicle to send a string of buoyant tunes up the charts. The albums *Here Where There Is Love* and *The Windows of the World* generate the hits *Alfie* and *I Say a Little Prayer*, among others. The fiery "Queen of Soul," ARETHA FRANKLIN's raw, gospel-tinged vocals fuel her meteoric rise to the top. Her LPs *I Never Loved a Man (The Way I Love You)* and *Aretha Arrives* are a mine of huge hits, including *(You Make Me Feel Like) A Natural Woman, Chain of Fools* and the #1 record *Respect*.

A pair of seminal blues artists release influential albums. Electric guitar master **Albert King**'s *Born Under a Bad Sign* contains the title track plus King's scorching rendition of *Crosscut Saw*. **John Lee Hooker**'s *Urban Blues* includes the foot-stomping boogie *Boom Boom Boom*. Both records provide the raw material for countless future blues and rock interpretations.

STAX Records, and it's subsidiary **VOLT**, has a big year, challenging **MOTOWN** Records for parity in the Soul/R&B arena. Memphis keyboardist **Booker T. Jones** and his band, the **MG's**, combine with **Mar-Keys** guitarist **Steve Cropper** and bassist **Duck Dunn** to solidify the signature "Stax Sound," boosting the label to success with hits by **Otis Redding** (*Try a Little Tenderness, Shake*), **Wilson Pickett** (*Funky Broadway*) and **Sam & Dave** (*Soul Man*). Hit machine Motown stumbles a bit when its primary songwriters **Lamont Dozier** and brothers **Brian Holland** and **Edward Holland** depart amid financial acrimony. Nevertheless, Motown mogul **Berry Gordy** signs **Gladys Knight and the Pips** while label stalwarts **The Four Tops** score hits with *Bernadette* and *I Got a Feeling*, as do **Diana Ross and the Supremes** with *Love Is Here and Now You're Gone* and *The Happening*.

Booker T. & the MG's: l-r Donald "Duck" Dunn, Booker T. Jones, Steve Cropper, Al Jackson

A young Wilson Pickett

Diana Ross (top) and the Supremes

30

Jazz

The first annual **Montreux Jazz Festival** takes place in Switzerland. Participants over the 3 days include **Charles Lloyd**, **Keith Jarrett**, **Bill Evans**, **Nina Simone** and **Ella Fitzgerald**.

The double live LP *Ella (Fitzgerald) & Duke (Ellington) at The Cote D'Azur* swings madly and features Ella's driving take on *Mack the Knife*.

Ever-evolving trumpeter **Miles Davis** releases two albums: *Sorcerer* and *Nefertiti*. He is backed on both by his working band of the moment: **Wayne Shorter** (s), **Herbie Hancock** (p), **Ron Carter** (b) and **Tony Williams** (d). Shorter's arresting compositions provide the bulk of the material. A portrait of Miles' 2nd wife, actress **Cicely Tyson**, graces the cover of *Sorcerer*.

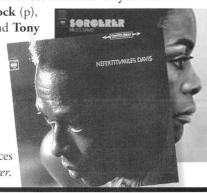

Veteran producer **Creed Taylor** launches CTI Records. The label's releases are often characterized by lush orchestrations and striking gatefold album covers featuring **Pete Turner** photographs. **Wes Montgomery**, **Herbie Mann**, **Antonio Carlos Jobim** and **George Benson** are some of the first artists affiliated with CTI.

The New Thing

While much of the audience for popular music remains transfixed by the rapidly developing currents in rock and R&B, an array of musicians—largely elaborating on the explorations of saxophonist **John Coltrane**—push jazz to the extremes of free form and collective improvisation. Decisively uncommercial and increasingly Afrocentric, "free jazz" initially sounds imposingly dissonant and dense. But close listening reveals a music rooted in historical tradition, created by impassioned, disciplined performers. Notable contributors include saxophonists **Archie Shepp**, **Albert Ayler** and **Pharoah Sanders**, pianist **Cecil Taylor**, trombonist **Roswell Rudd**, drummer **Ed Blackwell**, and bassists **Charlie Haden** and **Reggie Workman**.

Above, Archie Shepp's 1967 Magic of Ju Ju LP. Right, Pharoah Sanders plays soprano saxophone with Reggie Workman on bass.

downbeat Critics' Poll

Hall of Fame **Bessie Smith**
Jazz Album of the Year **Duke Ellington** *The Popular Ellington*
Big Band **Duke Ellington**
Acoustic Jazz Group **Miles Davis**
Alto Saxophone **Ornette Coleman**
Tenor Saxophone **Sonny Rollins**
Baritone Saxophone **Harry Carney**
Trumpet **Miles Davis**
Trombone **J.J. Johnson**
Clarinet **Pee Wee Russell**
Drums **Elvin Jones**
Vibes **Milt Jackson**
Acoustic Bass **Richard Davis**
Guitar **Wes Montgomery**
Piano **Earl Hines**
Organ **Jimmy Smith**
Miscellaneous Instrument **Roland Kirk-** Manzello & Stritch
Arranger **Duke Ellington**
Composer **Duke Ellington**
Male Vocalist **Louis Armstrong**
Female Vocalist **Ella Fitzgerald**

Wes Montgomery

a cool breeze

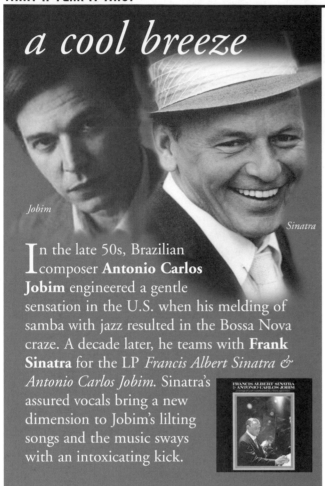

Jobim

Sinatra

In the late 50s, Brazilian composer **Antonio Carlos Jobim** engineered a gentle sensation in the U.S. when his melding of samba with jazz resulted in the Bossa Nova craze. A decade later, he teams with **Frank Sinatra** for the LP *Francis Albert Sinatra & Antonio Carlos Jobim*. Sinatra's assured vocals bring a new dimension to Jobim's lilting songs and the music sways with an intoxicating kick.

BORN IN 1967 ★
KURT COBAIN
HARRY CONNICK JR.
BILLY CORGAN
FAITH HILL
DAVE MATTHEWS
DAVE NAVARRO
MOON ZAPPA

Kurt Cobain

Alto saxist **Julian "Cannonball" Adderley** has a hit with the million-selling instrumental **Mercy, Mercy, Mercy**, written by Joe Zawinul.

Louis Armstrong records **What a Wonderful World.**

The music world says goodbye to:

Saxophonist **JOHN COLTRANE** (40) dies of liver cancer at the peak of his powers. One of the pivotal artists in American music history, he fundamentally altered the perception of the saxophone and the improvisational solo. His increasingly lengthy, complex and unrestrained musical statements laid the groundwork for free jazz and would influence countless artists.

Beatles' manager **BRIAN EPSTEIN** (32) dies of a drug overdose.

WOODY GUTHRIE (55) succumbs to the degenerative disease Huntington's Chorea. Bob Dylan, who visited the folk singer in his final days, called him "my last hero." Through his ballads, Guthrie chronicled the dustbowl, championed the downtrodden and fought fascism. He is best remembered for his anthemic *This Land is Your Land*.

Soul singer **OTIS REDDING** (26) dies in an airplane crash three days after recording his biggest hit *(Sittin' on) the Dock of the Bay*.

Composer and pianist **BILLY STRAYHORN** (51) dies of esophageal cancer. His collaboration and close friendship with Duke Ellington yielded a legacy of enduring music, including *Take the 'A' Train*.

PAUL WHITEMAN (77), the self-styled "King of Jazz," was an immensely successful and popular orchestra leader in the 20s and 30s.

John Coltrane

Woody Guthrie

COUNTRY & WESTERN

BIG HITS

Former studio pro **GLEN CAMPBELL** breaks through with the smash *Gentle on My Mind*, which earns a total of 4 Grammy Awards for Glen and the song's composer, **John Hartford**.

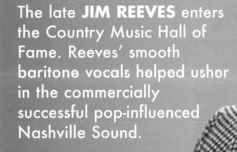

The late **JIM REEVES** enters the Country Music Hall of Fame. Reeves' smooth baritone vocals helped usher in the commercially successful pop-influenced Nashville Sound.

Campbell

Best known as a songwriter, **DOLLY PARTON** *emerges as a country singer with the hits* **Dumb Blonde** *and* The Last Thing on My Mind *(a duet with Porter Wagoner). She also has success with her first solo album,* Hello I'm Dolly.

Merle Haggard is an exponent of the "Bakersfield Sound" who, along with his band **the Strangers**, is instrumental in bringing hard-picking electric guitar to the forefront in country music. *Music City News* names him Country Male Artist of the Year and the Academy of Country Music honors him for Top Vocal Duet (with **Bonnie Owens**). His album *Branded Man* is a good seller as are the singles *The Fugitive* and *Branded Man*.

Merle Haggard and The Strangers
Branded Man

Johnny Cash and **June Carter Cash** record their raucous duet, **Jackson**.

Don't Come Home a' Drinkin' (With Lovin' On Your Mind)
Loretta Lynn

Loretta Lynn

I Won't Come in While He's There
Jim Reeves

Walk Through This World With Me
George Jones

Lonely Again
Eddy Arnold

Sam's Place
Buck Owens & the Buckaroos

It's Such a Pretty World Today
Wynn Stewart

Tonight Carmen
Marty Robbins

I'll Never Find Another You / It's the Little Things
Sonny James

You Mean the World to Me
David Houston

I Don't Wanna Play House
Tammy Wynette

Tammy Wynette

GRAMMY awards

Bobbie Gentry

Lou Rawls

Record of the Year
UP, UP AND AWAY
5th Dimension

Song of the Year
UP, UP AND AWAY
Jimmy L. Webb, writer

Album of the Year
SGT. PEPPER'S LONELY HEARTS CLUB BAND
The Beatles

Vocal Performance, Female
ODE TO BILLIE JOE
Bobbie Gentry

Vocal Performance, Male
BY THE TIME I GET TO PHOENIX
Glen Campbell

New Artist
BOBBIE GENTRY

Rhythm & Blues Recording
RESPECT
Aretha Franklin

Rhythm & Blues Vocal, Female
RESPECT
Aretha Franklin

Rhythm & Blues Vocal, Male
DEAD END STREET
Lou Rawls

Rhythm & Blues Group, Vocal or Instrumental
SOUL MAN
Sam & Dave

Jazz Performance, Small Group
MERCY, MERCY, MERCY
Cannonball Adderly

Jazz Performance, Large Group
FAR EAST SUITE
Duke Ellington

Country & Western Song
GENTLE ON MY MIND
John Hartford, writer

Country & Western Recording
GENTLE ON MY MIND
Glen Campbell

Folk Performance
GENTLE ON MY MIND
John Hartford

Album of the Year, Classical
Mahler, SYMPHONY No. 8
Leonard Bernstein conducting
London Symphony Orchestra

Classical Performance, Orchestra
Stravinsky, FIREBIRD & PETROUCHKA
Igor Stravinsky
Columbia Symphony Orchestra

Comedy Performance
REVENGE
Bill Cosby

Some of the portable people don't know that Toshiba is here! (please tell them)

We make a special kind of portable. They're created inside and out to take the jolts and jars portable people give them.

Color TV with a brilliant, new Toshiba rectangular picture tube bonded to steel bands. Solid state circuitry that stays put and performs.

We modestly claim to be the world's largest producer of transistors and diodes for the home entertainment field. You'll never see our portable people at the drug store tube-testing machine.

How about portable radios with handles that don't come off in your hands? Or sound that won't wear out before your second set of batteries. They are Toshiba Duraligned, precision crafted to do just that.

And they are warranteed for *one full year parts and labor.*

World travelers know the reputation of Toshiba, The International One, in 130 countries. (They write our best ads.) Now we're at most fine quality stores across the USA. No jet trip necessary to join the ranks of the portable people.

So please tell the portable people we're here. It'll be a nice thing to do for them and us. Thanks.

Toshiba. THE INTERNATIONAL ONE

Bottom to Top: All Solid State. The Surfer, Battery/Plug-in Portable TV. 37 sq. in. picture $139.50* • The Global, 7 Band Solid State Shortwave/FM/AM 2-in-1 $180.00* The Londonaire, Worlds Thinnest Solid State shirt pocket FM/AM. $34.50* The Stockholm, Solid State 3 Band Marine Shortwave FM/AM 2-in-1 $64.50* • *Mfg. suggested retail price.

ORCHESTRA NEWS

Classical Music

Strauss memorial statue in Vienna's City Park

THE VIENNA PHILHARMONIC, the oldest symphonic orchestra with a record of continual performance, celebrates its 125th anniversary with an American tour. It joins the NEW YORK PHILHARMONIC—which reaches its 125th birthday in the same year—for their season opener. The ISRAEL PHILHARMONIC also visits the U.S., following Israel's decisive victory in the Six Day War.

The New York Philharmonic has just negotiated a contract making it the highest paid orchestra in the U.S. Its weekly broadcasts, however, come to a close. The New York Philharmonic is also seeking a new conductor, as are the BOSTON and CHICAGO Orchestras.

Andre Previn becomes conductor of the HOUSTON SYMPHONY, saying he has "made the choice between Debbie Reynold's movies and Gustav Mahler's music." Meanwhile, the Cleveland Orchestra, youngest of the best American ensembles, opens its 50th season.

Previn

Leonard Bernstein, director of the NY Philharmonic, proclaims: *"What I like of the new pop music is maybe 5 percent of the whole output... it's mostly trash. But that 5 percent is so exciting, and... so significant, that it claims the attention of every thinking person."*

NEW COMPOSITIONS

Penderecki

Polish composer **Krzysztof Penderecki**'s 1965 *St. Luke's Passion* wins the 1967 Prix Italia and he completes his new installment, the choral work *Dies Irae* (Day of Wrath), dedicated to the victims of Auschwitz.

Briton **William Walton**'s one-act comic opera, *The Bear*, is well received at the Aldeburgh Festival.

Leon Kirchner's *Quartet No. 3* debuts at Town Hall with the Beaux Arts Quartet in January, and wins the Pulitzer Prize for music.

Walton

NOTABLE NEW LPS

Hector Berlioz: REQUIEM
Charles Munch
Orchester des Bayerischen and Chorus

Honneger: JOAN OF ARC AT THE STAKE
Seiji Ozawa
London Symphony Orchestra and Chorus

SILVER APPLES OF THE MOON
Morton Subotnick

A series of concerts celebrate the 100th anniversary of ARTURO TOSCANINI'S birth.

36

MET METROPOLITAN OPERA

MOURNING BECOMES ELECTRA

Opera News

Below, Zubin Mehta, top, and Eugene O'Neill. At left, Evelyn Lear and Marie Collier.

New York's **Metropolitan Opera** premieres *Mourning Becomes Electra*, based on American playwright **Eugene O'Neill**'s version of the Electra legend. Set in post Civil War New England, **Marvin David Levy**'s opera presents **Marie Collier** and **Evelyn Lear** in their Met debuts, with support from **John Reardon** and **Sherrill Milnes**. **Zubin Mehta** conducts.

Having completed its first season in New York City's Lincoln Center for the Performing Arts—the longest season in its history—the Met exceeds its fund-raising drive of $3,000,000 by $500,000.

Other companies are not so fortunate. Chicago's **Lyric Opera** cancels its season because of union troubles, and the **Lake Erie Opera Theater** in Cleveland, Ohio, also faces a union problem. Meanwhile, the **Santa Fe Opera**'s home theater is destroyed in a fire in July.

Herbert von Karajan conducts **Verdi**'s *Requiem* at La Scala, Milan, in a production many regard as one of the finest ever seen. Soprano **Leontyne Price** is joined by young tenor **Luciano Pavarotti**, and French filmmaker **Henri George Clouzot** records the event for posterity. *Price*

Finland's Savonlinna Opera Festival resumes after laying dormant for nearly 4 decades. Presented in the courtyard of medieval Olavinlinna Castle, **Beethoven**'s *Fidelio* is the first new offering.

Olavinlinna Castle

The Metropolitan Opera's Road Company is discontinued, replaced by the American National Opera Company headed by **Sarah Caldwell**.

PASSINGS

Scottish operatic soprano **MARY GARDEN** (92), who created a sensation as Salomé, is remembered as the embodiment of the "Diva" stereotype.

Singer and film star **NELSON EDDY** (65) is fondly recalled for his duets with Jeanette MacDonald.

Pablo Casals is 90

The world famous cellist and composer begins his 90th birthday by attending mass at Our Lady of Mercy church nearby his Isla Verde, Puerto Rico home. He is greeted by the Archbishop of San Juan.

Only a few intimate friends are invited to the morning mass which includes music composed by Casals. During the service, the Archbishop extolls the virtues of Casals the man, the musician and the humanitarian.

Later, at home, Happy Birthday is sung in both English and Spanish. Scores of wires and letters are received, including one from U. S. President Lyndon Johnson reminiscing about a Casals recital at the White House. The world joins in toasting an immortal of the music world!

Dance

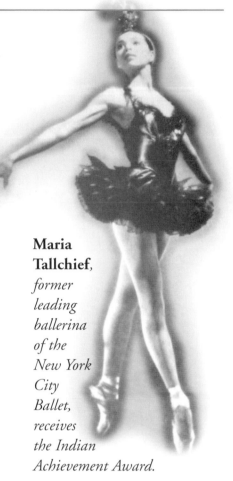

Maria Tallchief, *former leading ballerina of the New York City Ballet, receives the Indian Achievement Award.*

At New York State Theater, **George Balanchine**'s *Jewels* is the greatest success of the season for **The New York City Ballet**, while 24 of the company's dancers are the hit of the Edinburgh Festival in August. **The American Ballet Theater**, also appearing at the State Theater (while the **British Royal Ballet** performs next door), is the first U.S. company to perform the full-length *Swan Lake*.

Balanchine

At City Center, **Joffrey Ballet** offers *The Green Table* and *Astarte*.

Eliot Feld emerges as the next promising new choreographer.

Italian prima ballerina **Carla Fracci** makes her New York debut in *Giselle*, *La Sylphide*, and *Romeo and Juliet*.

The 35th Annual Summer Dance Festival is held at Jacob's Pillow in Lee, Massachusetts, and the American Dance Festival at Connecticut College celebrates its 20th anniversary.

CAPEZIO AWARD	GRAND PRIX ITALIA
Paul Taylor	Alvin Ailey

NEW POPULAR DANCES
The Camel Walk, The Boogaloo, and Monkey Jive

Bolshoi Ballet 67 *offers American moviegoers an intimate look at one of the U.S.S.R.'s most sacred cultural institutions through the eyes of an aspiring young ballerina.*

The Berlin Staatsballett production of *The Sleeping Beauty* premieres in October 1967.

Don't dare use Hai Karate

without memorizing this

Here are step-by-step instructions on how to defend yourself from women in case you find yourself in a tight squeeze because you applied an overdose of Hai Karate Oriental Lime.

1. When your girl (or even your own wife) gets to squeezing too hard, force your arms under hers with your palms facing one another.

2. Take a deep breath and push both arms skyward vigorously while springing from the knees.

3. Now her hold is broken. Get her in a good, tight half nelson and shock her back to reality with a stern warning such as, "Watch it, Sister!"

Limes are for squeezing. So you can imagine what can happen if you use too much Hai Karate Oriental Lime After Shave. Or Lime Cologne. Your girl can get carried away. And do squeezy things to you.

That's why we put these instructions on self defense in every package. Just like we do in regular Hai Karate.

If you know what's good for you, you'll memorize them right now.

HAI KARATE be careful how you use it.

40

ON BROADWAY

JUDY
LIGHTS UP THE GREAT WHITE WAY

Singer JUDY GARLAND takes up residence at Broadway's Palace Theatre for a four-week run, wowing crowds and critics alike. Her comeback show is a vaudeville style presentation whose centerpiece concert features the songs with which she has come to be associated, including *The Man That Got Away, What Now My Love, Chicago* and *Rockabye My Baby*.

MARLENE DIETRICH settles in for a 6-week engagement at Broadway's Lunt-Fontanne Theatre. The German-born actress/singer delves deeply into the repertoire of the songs, *lieder* and *chansons* she made famous as a cabaret performer and in her many Hollywood and European movies. Defying her 66 years, Dietrich looks fit and glamorous in a tight silver dress. **Burt Bacharach** handles the arranging and conducting.

Singer **Eddie Fisher** and comedian **Buddy Hackett** are at the Palace Theatre for a 5-week run.

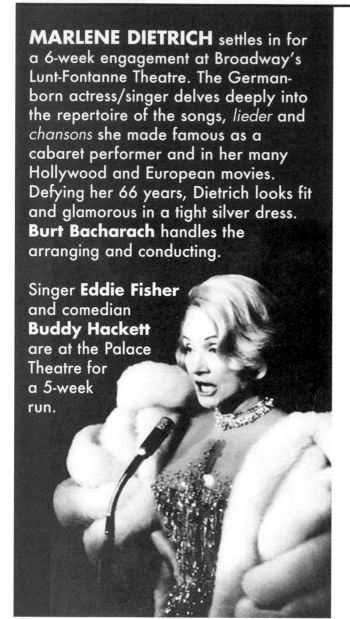

THE DEVILS, starring **Frank Langella**, is the first production of the Mark Taper Forum in Los Angeles. The play is adapted from **Aldous Huxley**'s book, *The Devils of Loudon*, which recounts the true story of a priest and a "possessed" order of nuns. *The Devils* proceeds despite the expressed misgivings of the Los Angeles County Board of Supervisors and the Archdiocese over the strong sexual content and perceived anti-Catholicism of the material.

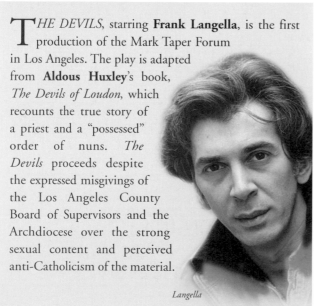

Langella

dolly'll never go away

Martha Raye

So successful is the musical smash **HELLO, DOLLY!** that it engenders a cottage industry of sorts. The original Broadway production at the St. James Theater, which opened in January 1964, will eventually run for 2,844 performances while simultaneously playing on tour in the U.S. and abroad. Over its course, nine different actresses will play Mrs. Dolly Levi Gallagher, the role originally portrayed by **Carol Channing**. In 1967 alone **Martha Raye**, **Betty Grable** and **Bibi Osterwald** undertake the role, as well as **Pearl Bailey**, who headlines an all-black "Dolly" along with **Cab Calloway**.

Pearl Bailey and Cab Calloway

Not quite so long-lived is Spike Jones' band alumnus **Mickey Katz'** "Borschtcapade" satire, **HELLO, SOLLY!** The English-Yiddish revue manages 2 months at the Henry Miller Theater.

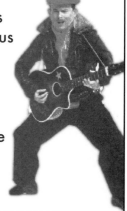

Katz

Gary Burghoff

new musicals

The March 17 cover of *Life* magazine featuring cartoonist **Charles M. Schulz**' beloved characters underneath the headline, "Charlie Brown and Snoopy: Winners at Last," is the latest evidence that the comic strip *Peanuts* gang has become a near national obsession. Broadway's part in the frenzy is the musical **YOU'RE A GOOD MAN CHARLIE BROWN**. Written in its entirety by **Clark Gesner**, the production promises "a peek into an average day in the life of Charlie Brown." With **Gary Burghoff** in the title role, Snoopy fighting the Red Baron atop his doghouse and amusing songs like *My Blanket and Me, The Doctor Is In* and *Beethoven Day,* audiences are won over and the show enjoys a good run.

An affirmation of the counterculture through a story involving drugs, Vietnam politics, flag desecration and hippies, much of it performed in the nude, **HAIR**—subtitled *The American Tribal Love-Rock Musical*—creates a stir even in its initial performances at a New York go-go club called the Cheetah. Written by **James Rado** and **Gerome Ragni** (book and lyrics), and **Galt MacDermot** (music), *Hair* quickly moves to an off-Broadway location on its way to becoming an international sensation. The controversy over *Hair* may have amounted to little if not for a lot of very good songs in the show, many of which subsequently hit the pop charts, including *Hair, Where Do I Go?, Easy to Be Hard, Aquarius* and *Good Morning Starshine.*

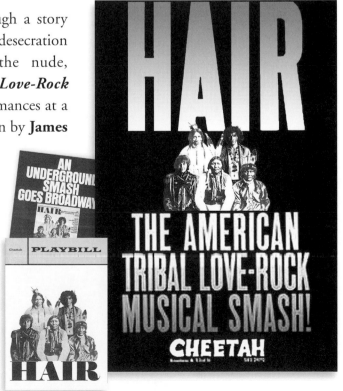

SHOWS OPEN

After the Rain

The Birthday Party

Black Comedy / White Lies

The East Wind

The Girl in the Freudian Slip

Hallelujah, Baby!

Halfway Up the Tree

The Homecoming

Illya Darling

The Imaginary Invalid

Keep It In the Family

Little Murders

Of Love Remembered

The Paisley Convertible

The Promise

Rosencrantz and Guildenstern Are Dead

A Touch of the Poet

The Wild Duck

You Can't Take It With You

There's a Girl in My Soup

Ian Holm & Vivien Merchant

British playwright **Harold Pinter** stirs controversy with his avant-garde play **THE HOMECOMING**, which centers on a university professor named Teddy (**Ian Holm**) and his wife (**Vivien Merchant**), who pay a visit to his abusive family. Degradation, insult and verbal violence ensue, driving the shamed Teddy away while his sexually humiliated wife opts to stay behind with the all-male family members.

- *CURLEY McDIMPLE*, featuring **Bernadette Peters** in one of her earliest roles, opens off-Broadway at the Bert Wheeler Theatre in November.

- The controversial off-Broadway play *MacBIRD!* by **Barbara Garson** is a political satire based on *Macbeth* which has the Vice President taking the country's top job after the President is assassinated.

- *Finian's Rainbow* is revived by New York's City Center in April.

Jules Dassin based the musical **ILLYA DARLING** on his film, *Never on Sunday*. The ribald stage production about a life-long prostitute in a Greek seaport features Dassin's wife **Melina Mercouri** in the title role and **Orson Bean** as Homer, an American intellectual.

Orson Bean (seated) and Melina Mercouri

Quayle and Herlie

Peter Ustinov's comedy **HALFWAY UP THE TREE**, "a farcical morality in three acts," stars **Anthony Quayle** as General Sir Mallalieu Fitzbuttress, fresh from military service in the Malayan jungles, who finds himself unable to cope with a series of domestic crises and decides to live in a tree. **Eileen Herlie** is his suffering wife.

SHOWS CLOSE

The Apple Tree

At the Drop of Another Hat

Barefoot in the Park

Brief Lives

By George

Come Live With Me

A Delicate Balance

Dinner at Eight

Funny Girl

The Impossible Years

The Killing of Sister George

The Natural Look

The Ninety Day Mistress

The Odd Couple

Sherry!

The Star-Spangled Girl

Sweet Charity

Wait a Minim

Walking Happy

A Warm Body

New York City creates the "Special Theatre District," recognizing the unique character of the Times Square area.

on-going productions

Robert Preston & Mary Martin in I Do! I Do!
Herschel Bernardi in Fiddler on the Roof.
Chita Rivera in Sweet Charity *(Boston).*

46

The London Stage

The first professional production of *Rosencrantz & Guildenstern Are Dead* is on April 11 at the Old Vic Theatre in London, by the National Theatre Company.

Oliver! opens at the Piccadilly Theatre in April.

The Boy Friend with **Sandy Wilson** opens at the Comedy Theatre in London and runs for 365 performances.

The London production of *Fiddler On The Roof* opens at Her Majesty's Theatre and runs for 2,030 performances.

The Four Musketeers opens in London at the Drury Lane Theatre.

Sweet Charity opens at the Prince Of Wales Theatre in London.

EDWARD ALBEE is awarded the PULITZER PRIZE for best original American play, *A Delicate Balance*.

FINAL CURTAIN

Rains

CLAUDE RAINS (78), whose Broadway role in *Darkness at Noon* won him the New York Drama Critics Circle best actor award and whose lengthy movie career brought him 4 Oscar® nominations.

BASIL RATHBONE (75), who played on Broadway in *The Barretts of Wimpole Street*, *The Heiress*, and *Obsession* as well as in many films, often as Sherlock Holmes.

For the first time, the annual Antoinette Perry (Tony) Awards ceremony is produced as a national television special, airing on CBS-TV.

TONY AWARDS

PLAY	*The Homecoming*
MUSICAL	*Cabaret*
ACTOR/PLAY	**Paul Rogers** *The Homecoming*
ACTRESS/PLAY	**Beryl Reid** *The Killing of Sister George*
SUPPORTING ACTOR	**Ian Holm** *The Homecoming*
SUPPORTING ACTRESS	**Marian Seldes** *A Delicate Balance*
ACTOR/ MUSICAL	**Robert Preston** *I Do! I Do!*
ACTRESS/ MUSICAL	**Barbara Harris** *The Apple Tree*
DIRECTOR/ PLAY	**Peter Hall** *The Homecoming*
DIRECTOR/ MUSICAL	**Harold S. Prince** *Cabaret*

The skier flies downhill so fast
That no one's ever passed 'er,
And only our Tomato Soup
Has ever gone down faster!

You always eat better with *Campbell's*

ART

Minimalism reaches its peak, coinciding with the lionization and August death of the movement's godfather, painter **AD REINHARDT**, who is celebrated in a splashy *Life* magazine spread and a retrospective last year at New York's Jewish Museum. Known for his monochromatic and black works, Reinhardt espoused his rules for purity in painting, including the things artists must avoid: texture, brushwork, drawing, forms, design, color, subjects and images. As for sculpture, Reinhardt had little use for it, calling it "...something you bump into when you back up to look at a painting."

Reinhardt

Reinhardt's acolytes continue in their quest to reduce painting to the essentials of geometric abstraction rendered with an extreme economy of means and color, **Sol LeWitt** and **Frank Stella** among them. Reinhardt's joke notwithstanding, there *are* minimalist sculptors such as **Donald Judd** and **Carl Andre** who persist in making works which are flat or cubic and seamless, often hugging the floor or claiming the corner. And **Dan Flavin** continues his light explorations utilizing configurations of bare flourescent tubes.

Untitled *1967, Stainless steel. Sculpture by Donald Judd*

The Chicago Museum of Contemporary Art opens, attracting 3,000 members in its first year. And at Chicago's Daley Center Plaza, a monumental steel sculpture by **Pablo Picasso** is unveiled. Standing 50 feet tall and weighing 162 tons, the sculpture's design is a gift from the artist to the people of Chicago.

- A major exhibition of Picasso sculpture and ceramics opens at London's Tate Gallery, then travels to New York's Museum of Modern Art.

The Metropolitan Museum of Art discovers 40,000 prints and negatives, representing much of the work of photographer **JAMES VAN DER ZEE**, and displays many of them in its *Harlem on My Mind* exhibition.

49

The National Gallery of Art in Washington, D.C., spends $5 million—the largest sum ever paid for a work of art —to buy Ginevra de' Benci, the only painting by LEONARDO DA VINCI in the Western Hemisphere and the first of only three known portraits he painted of women; the others are Mona Lisa in Paris and Woman with an Ermine in Krakow.

Artist FRANK STELLA begins his "Protractor" series of paintings and prints.

Video art pioneer **Nam June Paik** stages his *Opera Sextronique* in which cellist **Charlotte Moorman** plays while clad in a battery-powered bra with small televisions covering her nipples, accompanied by the "Young Penis Symphony." Before Moorman can begin a portion of her performance in which she is to appear topless, New York police interrupt, arresting her and Paik.

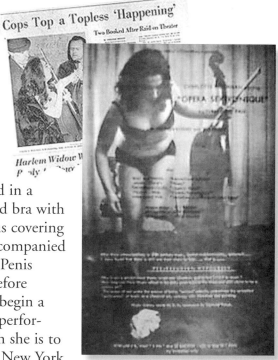

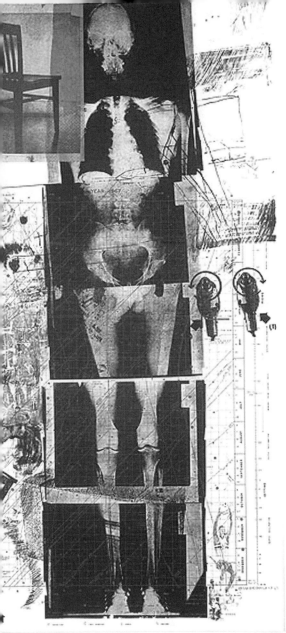

Andy Warhol

The rock album ***The Velvet Underground & Nico*** sports a cover by **ANDY WARHOL**. A banana with the notation "peel slowly and see" can actually be "peeled," revealing pink-colored fruit beneath its paper skin.

ANDY WARHOL shows in the Whitney Museum of American Art's 1967 Annual exhibition.

The Los Angeles fine print studio Gemini G.E.L. produces **Robert Rauschenberg**'s *Booster*, the largest lithograph ever printed on a hand operated lithographic press. The piece incorporates life-size x-rays of the artist's body as well as his characteristic transfers and drawings.

CHRISTO completes *Corridor Store Front, 1967*, wherein he wraps 1,500 square feet of storefront surface in fabric and paper.

PASSINGS

Magritte's The Betrayal of Images

Watercolorist **CHARLES BURCHFIELD** (73) was known for his fantastic, almost hallucinogenic landscapes.

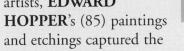

Ceci n'est pas une pipe.

One of America's most famous and popular artists, **EDWARD HOPPER**'s (85) paintings and etchings captured the stark solitude of American urban and rural life.

Belgian surrealist painter **René Magritte** (69) dies.

Hopper's Nighthawks

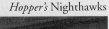

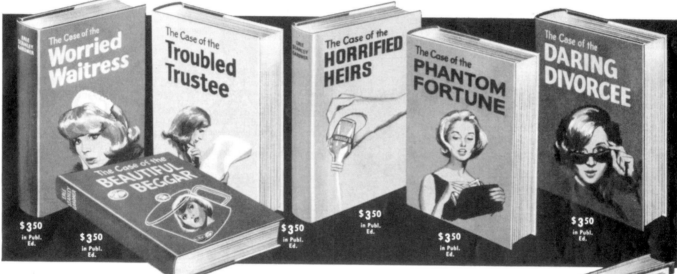
52

Books

Marshall **McLuhan**'s *The Medium is the Massage: An Inventory of Effects* is published by Bantam and becomes an instant classic. McLuhan's analysis and philosophy of mass media and its effect on society is elucidated through an innovative juxtaposition of text and graphics. The originally intended title, *The Medium is the Message*, is altered through a printer's error. McLuhan considers the mistake a happy accident and keeps the title as is.

A study of human behavior from a zoologist's perspective, **Desmond Morris**' *The Naked Ape* shocks some with the conclusions drawn by its comparison of humans and apes. Nevertheless, the frank look at *homo sapiens* "...feeding, sleeping, fighting, mating and rearing young" is an international bestseller.

Richard **Brautigan**'s novel, *Trout Fishing in America* is really a collection of short episodes chronicling his travels through the country and the yearning for a simpler, more human America. One critic says Brautigan is "like Ernest Hemingway but with the disillusioned eyes of a flower child." Though not his first book, "Trout Fishing" makes a major cult figure of Brautigan.

Franz Kafka is frequently invoked to describe **Susan Sontag**'s second novel, the dark, dreamlike *Death Kit*. Less experimental but no less thought-provoking is **Norman Mailer**'s *Why Are We in Vietnam?* It too is a meditation on society, life and death, but through the eyes of an American teenager about to go to war.

Just for laughs comes *Misery Is a Blind Date* by **Johnny Carson,** and *Marriage Manual* by **Phyllis Diller**. Diller advises "never refer to your wedding night as the original Amateur Hour."

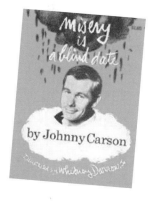

Craig Rodwell opens "Oscar Wilde's," the first gay bookstore in lower Manhattan.

Eventual winner of the Nobel Prize for Literature, Soviet dissident author **Alexander Solzhenitsyn** meets **Olga Andreyev Carlisle** in Moscow. With the KGB seizing Solzhenitsyn's papers, Carlisle agrees to smuggle manuscripts of **The First Circle** and **The Gulag Archipelago** to the West, leading to their publication and the exposure of Soviet atrocities.

Aldous Huxley

Books

Gabriel García Márquez

All the Little Things
Wallace Stegner

•

The Arrangement
Elia Kazan

•

A Bad Man
Stanley Elkins

•

The Chosen
Chaim Potok

•

Christy
Catherine Marshall

•

The Confessions of Nat Turner
William Styron

•

The Crisis of the Negro Intellectual
Harold Cruse

•

The Crows of Pearblossom
Aldous Huxley

Death of a President
William Manchester

•

Division Street: America
Studs Terkel

•

The Eighth Day
Thornton Wilder

•

Everything But Money
Sam Levenson

•

The Exhibitionist
Henry Sutton

•

The Gabriel Hounds
Mary Stewart

•

Games People Play
Eric Berne, M.D.

•

Jerusalem the Golden
Margaret Drabble

•

Killing Time
Thomas Berger

A Modern Priest Looks at His Out-Dated Church
Father James Kavanaugh

•

One Hundred Years of Solitude
Gabriel García Márquez

•

Our Crowd
Stephen Birmingham

•

Rosemary's Baby
Ira Levin

•

The Sorrow Dance
Denise Levertov

•

Topaz
Leon Uris

•

Where Eagles Dare
Alistair MacLean

•

Wild Season
Allan W. Eckert

The American Library Association (ALA) *votes to keep their headquarters in Chicago. In addition, the ALA contributes about $11,000 to help libraries in Florence, Italy following the damaging flood in 1966.*

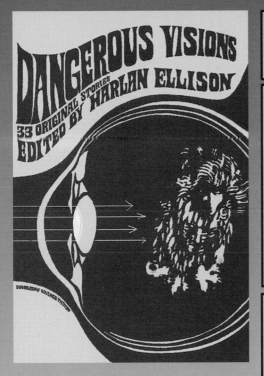

Asturias

Nobel Prize for Literature
Miguel Angel Asturias, Guatemala

Pulitzer Prizes

FICTION
The Fixer   Bernard Malamud

BIOGRAPHY
Mr. Clemens and Mark Twain   Justin Kaplan

POETRY
Live or Die   Anne Sexton

Hugo Award (Science Fiction)
The Moon Is A Harsh Mistress Robert A. Heinlein

Nebula Award
The Einstein Intersection Samuel R. Delany

Newbery Medal (Children's)
Up a Pond Slowly Irene Hunt

Prix Goncourt
La Marge Andre Pieyre de Mandiargues

Viareggio Prize
Il gabbiano azzurro Raffaello Brignetti

Dangerous Visions, *a sci-fi short story anthology edited by* **Harlan Ellison**, *is published, and both the stories and anthology will receive awards the following year. Ellison garners a special citation at the 26th World Science Fiction Convention for editing "the most significant and controversial Science Fiction book published in 1967."*

Farewell and Good Night:

Poet **JAMES LANGSTON HUGHES** dies of cancer at age 65. His first published poem is also one of his most famous, *The Negro Speaks of Rivers*. His poems, short plays, essays and short stories also appear in the NAACP's *Crisis Magazine* and in *Opportunity* magazine. Across his career, Hughes wrote sixteen books of poems, two novels, three collections of short stories, four volumes of "editorial" and "documentary" fiction, twenty plays, children's poetry, musicals and operas, three autobiographies, a dozen radio and television scripts and dozens of magazine articles.

Hughes

American novelist **CARSON McCULLERS** (*The Heart Is a Lonely Hunter*) dies at age 50 from a stroke.

Humorist **DOROTHY PARKER** (73) was known for her biting wit and sarcasm in short stories and poems which often appeared in magazines like the *New Yorker* and *Vanity Fair*. She was associated with the group of writers and wits who lunched regularly at New York's Algonquin Hotel.

Poet and novelist **CARL SANDBURG** dies of a heart attack in Flat Rock, North Carolina, at age 89. President Johnson calls him "the bard of democracy, the echo of the people."

Parker

The Trimline® phone. Scandalously easy to use.
The dial comes right to you. Table and wall models.
Six zingy colors. Extra long cord.

AT&T
and Associated Companies

In The News

U.S. troops assemble on a hilltop northeast of Dak To, Vietnam.

April 24, 1967—Operation Oregon, a search and destroy mission conducted by the infantry platoon of Troop B: a soldier is lowered into a tunnel by members of the reconnaissance platoon.

Right, above: U.S. President Lyndon Johnson decorates a soldier in a south Vietnam hospital.

Below: Vietnam War protestors mass outside White House gates, including Coretta Scott King and Dr. Benjamin Spock.

War Divides Two Nations

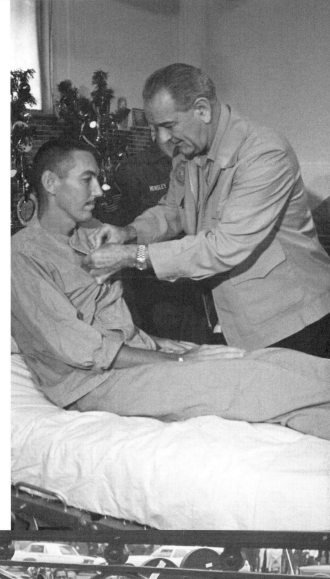

The Vietnam War—the longest war in U.S. history—continues abroad while Americans are increasingly polarized at home. 1967 opens with American forces in Vietnam numbering 385,000 plus 60,000 sailors stationed offshore. Casualty figures for the previous year show over 6,000 Americans killed and 30,000 wounded, with an estimated 61,000 Vietcong dead.

While soldiers fight, civilian protests grow and politicians debate. Speaking before the Senate, **George McGovern** (D-SD) says "We seem bent upon saving the Vietnamese from Ho Chi Minh, even if we have to kill them and demolish their country to do it." Publicly, U.S. National Security Advisor **Walt W. Rostow** remains optimistic: "I see a light at the end of the tunnel." But there is concern within President **Lyndon Johnson**'s administration. Secretary of Defense **Robert McNamara** testifies before a Senate subcommittee that U.S. bombing raids against North Vietnam have failed to achieve their objectives.

On the Tam Quan plain of South Vietnam,
OPERATION PERSHING
is a drive by U.S. 1st Cavalry soldiers determined to find and rout a huge Viet Cong force from the area.

A small village gives up enemy suspects who use grenades, automatic weapons and land mines to slow the advance of American cavalrymen. Unfortunately, peasant villagers are caught between the retreating guerillas and oncoming U.S. forces. The village is torched so that it cannot be used again as a base of operations for the VC.

A U.S. field hospital gives treatment to several women and children—tragic figures unfairly trapped in a war not of their making.

VIETNAM

JANUARY

U.S. Air Force F-4 Phantom jets shoot down seven North Vietnamese MiG-21 interceptors in a dogfight over Hanoi.

Operation Cedar Falls: American and South Vietnamese troops clear Viet Cong from the "Iron Triangle" area 25 miles northwest of Saigon. Allied troops uncover and destroy an extensive network of tunnels which the Viet Cong rebuild as soon as the area is vacated.

FEBRUARY Hostilities pause for a truce during Tet, the lunar New Year.

U.S. and South Vietnamese battalions launch the war's largest operation, Junction City, to destroy the North Vietnam Army's headquarters in South Vietnam. 2,728 Viet Cong are killed; 282 Americans are killed and 1,576 wounded.

MARCH 2,500 Viet Cong and NVA attack Quang Tri City.

U.S. bombers target Haiphong harbor in North Vietnam.

APRIL Fighting at Khe Sanh near Laos border results in 940 enemy killed. 155 Americans are killed.

MAY U.S. and South Vietnamese troops enter the Demilitarized Zone for the first time, engaging in firefights with NVA. Both sides suffer heavy losses.

JUNE U.S. Navy Swift Boats and Army troops deploy in Mekong Delta to halt Viet Cong usage of inland waterways.

JULY The USS Forestall catches fire in the Tonkin Gulf, killing 134 crewmen— the worst naval accident since World War II.

AUGUST U.S. discloses Laos Bombing.

SEPTEMBER National elections are held in South Vietnam with Nguyen Van Thieu elected president.

U.S. Marines are besieged at Con Thien, two miles south of the Demilitarized Zone.

OCTOBER The Battle of Dak To along the border of Cambodia and Laos preempts an NVA attack against Special Forces camps.

DECEMBER Battle of Tam Quan ends with 650 enemy + 58 U.S. dead.

Mass demonstrations in South Vietnam protest stepped-up Vietcong attacks, peace overtures by foreign politicians and reports of an exile government allegedly established in Paris. Targets include French President DeGaulle and U.S. Senators Fulbright and Robert Kennedy, who are publicly urging peace talks now.

THE WAR AT HOME

In his State of the Union address before a joint session of Congress, President **Lyndon B. Johnson** asks for a tax increase to fund the escalating Vietnam war.

"I recommend to the Congress a surcharge of 6% on both corporate and individual income taxes to last for two years or for so long as the unusual expenditures associated with our efforts in Vietnam continue."

JANUARY - U.N. Secretary-General U Thant expresses doubts that Vietnam is essential to the security of the West.

In his State of the Union address before Congress, **President Johnson** declares "We will stand firm in Vietnam."

FEBRUARY - Following the failure of diplomatic peace efforts, LBJ announces the U.S. will resume full-scale bombing of North Vietnam.

LBJ meets with advisors over lunch. Clockwise from left: McGeorge Bundy, Secy. Dean Rusk, LBJ, Secy. Paul Nitze, George Christian, Walt Rostow.

MARCH - President Johnson meets in Guam with South Vietnam's **Prime Minister Ky** and pressures Ky to hold national elections.

America's peace bid is rejected by **Ho Chi Minh**.

MAY - **Ellsworth Bunker** is appointed U.S ambassador to South Vietnam.

LBJ publicly urges North Vietnam to accept a peace compromise.

LBJ receives a warm welcome in Guam.

OCTOBER - LBJ reaffirms his commitment to maintain U.S. involvement in South Vietnam.

NOVEMBER - Following an optimistic White House briefing by **General William Westmoreland** and Ambassador Bunker, LBJ tells the American public on TV that progress is being made.

Robert McNamara resigns as Defense Secretary during a press briefing.

DECEMBER - LBJ makes his second and final presidential visit to Vietnam.

U.S. troop levels reach 463,000 with 16,000 combat deaths to date.

JANUARY - **Senator J. William Fulbright** publishes *The Arrogance of Power*, a book critical of American Vietnam policy, which advocates direct peace talks between the South Vietnamese government and the Viet Cong.

FEBRUARY - American religious groups stage a nationwide Fast for Peace.

APRIL - **Richard M. Nixon** says that anti-war protests in the U.S. are "prolonging the war."

Anti-war demonstrations in New York and San Francisco involve nearly 200,000.

Rev. Martin Luther King, Jr. declares that the war is undermining LBJ's Great Society social reform programs, and that the U.S. is "the greatest purveyor of violence in the world." He encourages draft resistance and suggests a merger between anti-war and civil rights groups.

General William Westmoreland condemns anti-war demonstrators, saying they give the North Vietnamese soldier "hope that he can win politically that which he cannot accomplish militarily." Privately, he has already warned President Johnson the war could go on indefinitely.

McCarthy, top, and Fulbright

Cassius Clay (Muhammad Ali) refuses military induction.

MAY - Famed philosopher and anti-war activist **Bertrand Russell** organizes a mock war-crimes tribunal in Stockholm which condemns the U.S.

AUGUST - California **Governor Ronald Reagan** says the U.S. should get out of Vietnam, citing the difficulties of winning a war when "too many qualified targets have been put off limits to bombing."

OCTOBER - March on the Pentagon draws 55,000 protesters. London protesters try to storm the U.S. embassy.

Anti-war Democrat **Eugene McCarthy** announces he will be a candidate for President against Lyndon Johnson.

DECEMBER - Four days of anti-war protests begin in New York. 585 protesters are arrested.

Veterans for Peace March on the Pentagon.

VP WELCOMES SENATORS

*In Washington, Vice President **Hubert Humphrey** (center) congratulates the freshman senators of the 90th Congress. The group includes **Charles Percy** of Illinois (third from right) and **Edward Brooke** of Massachusetts (far right)— the first African-American to be elected to the Senate by popular vote.*

GEORGIA CHOOSES SEGREGATIONIST

In Georgia, the state legislature settles the November election since neither of the gubernatorial candidates— **Lester Maddox** nor **Howard Callaway**—pulled more than 50% of the total. Lawmakers finally choose segregationist Maddox as governor. The former restaurant owner gained notoriety for his "Pickrick Drumsticks"— axe handles he and customers wielded at his Pickrick chicken eatery to defy the Civil Rights Bill of 1964 and keep blacks out.

Ebullient victor Maddox poses at legislature, above, signs axe handles, left.

The 25th Amendment to the United States Constitution is ratified, clarifying succession to the U.S. Presidency in case of the removal of the President or Vice President.

AMERICAN SAMOA's first constitution becomes effective on July 1, making it self-governing.

The body of President John F. Kennedy is moved from a temporary grave and interred in a permanent site at Arlington National Cemetery. The area is paved with irregular granite stones and an Eternal Flame burns from the center of a 5-foot circular flat granite stone located at the head of the President's grave.

The Long, Hot SUMMER

CITIES NATIONWIDE BURN WITH RACIAL UNREST

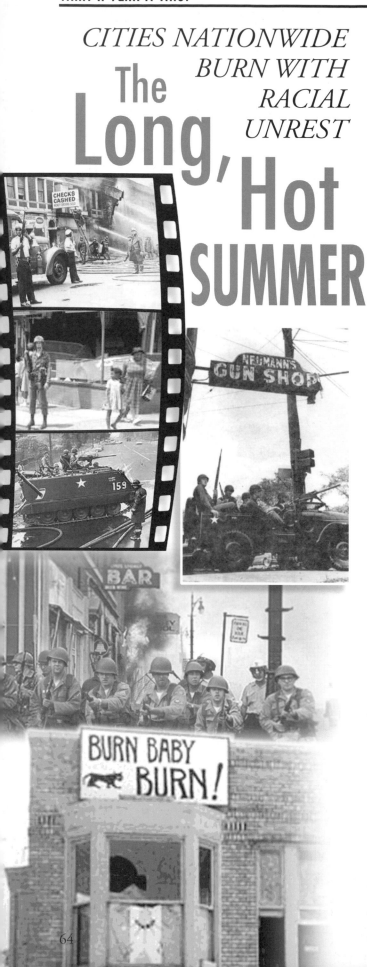

The cycle of black poverty, despair and urban turmoil—marked in the mid-sixties by the Harlem and Watts riots—reaches a crescendo, with violent outbreaks spreading across the country.

In Newark, New Jersey, reports of the unwarranted killing of a black taxi driver by a white police officer spark a riot commencing on July 14. The National Guard, called in to quell the uprising, is met by sniper fire and molotov cocktails. The event ends in 26 deaths, over 1,000 injuries and more than 1,400 arrests.

Days later, Detroit erupts in flames, violence and looting following a July 23 early morning police raid on a "blind pig"—an illegal saloon. The 5 days of the "12th Street Riot" are one of the most lethally destructive rebellions in modern America. Michigan Governor George Romney asks President Johnson to send in the National Guard. Before the Guard, army forces and Detroit police can restore calm, over 4,000 people are arrested, 2,500 stores are looted and/or burned, hundreds of families are displaced, hundreds are injured, and 43 people lose their lives.

Similar violent episodes rack the cities of Milwaukee, Buffalo, Tampa and others in the summer of 1967.

FBI Director J. Edgar Hoover (left) tells LBJ "outside agitators" play key roles in the year's race riots. Hoover orders counterintelligence officers to expose, disrupt, misdirect, and discredit the Black Panthers.

Nationwide rioting sparks the formation of President Johnson's National Advisory Commission on Civil Disorders, headed by Illinois Governor Otto Kerner. A Commission report states: "White racism is essentially responsible for the explosive mixture which has been accumulating in our cities since the end of World War II."

l-r: Roy Wilkins, Kerner, LBJ.

Solicitor General **THURGOOD MARSHALL** is nominated, confirmed and sworn in as the first African-American Justice of the United States Supreme Court. Marshall will go on to push for civil liberties and affirmative action.

CARL B. STOKES is elected mayor of Cleveland, Ohio, becoming the first African-American mayor of a major United States city.

In Macon County, Alabama, LUCIUS AMERSON becomes the first black sheriff in the south in the 20th century.

Gary, Indiana elects black mayor RICHARD HATCHER.

BLACKPANTHERS BLACKPOWER

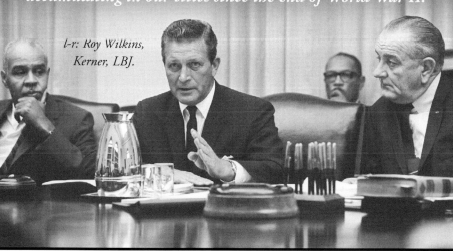

Angela Davi[s]

LIBERTAD PARA ANGELA DAV[IS]

30 armed members of the Black Panthers, including founders **Bobby Seale** and **Huey Newton**, march on the California State Capitol Building to protest gun-control legislation restricting the public display of firepower.

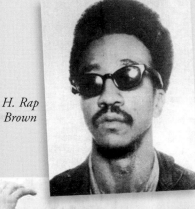

H. Rap Brown

Later in the year, Newton is charged with murder, intent to commit murder, and kidnapping following a traffic stop in Oakland, California involving the death of a police officer.

In front of an induction center in Georgia, **Stokely Carmichael**, chairman of the Student Nonviolent Coordinating Committee (SNCC), distributes antiwar flyers reading *"Receive valuable training in the skills of killing off other oppressed people!"* and *"You can't die fast enough in the ghettos."*

KIDNAPPED

Bobby Seale

H. Rap Brown, Carmichael's successor at SNCC, exhorts a crowd in Cambridge, Maryland, saying *"If America don't come around, we're going to burn America down!"* Several hours later, fire destroys a school and most of Cambridge's black businesses. Brown is arrested by the FBI, charged with "flight to escape prosecution for inciting arson in the city."

Stokely Carmichael

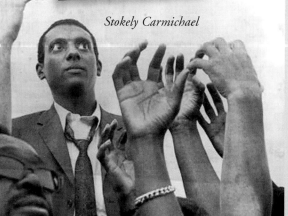

"It shall now be the policy of this state to immediately arrest any person inciting to riot, and to not allow that person to finish his vicious speech," says Maryland Governor **Spiro Agnew**.

Angela Davis joins SNCC and the Black Panther Party in 1967.

Huey Newton

65

ON CAPITOL HILL, the corruption controversy surrounding Congressman Adam Clayton Powell, Jr. comes to a head. Hundreds demonstrate in support of the Harlem Democrat who is removed from the Chairmanship of the Education and Labor Committee and is denied his House seat, pending an investigation. Powell comments, "Today marks the end of the U.S. as the land of the free and the home of the brave." Two years later, the Supreme Court will rule that the House had acted unconstitutionally when it excluded Powell.

IN A SURPRISE MOVE, New York Republicans choose civil rights figure James Meredith, who defied segregation to become the first black student at the University of Mississippi in 1962. He opposes Adam Clayton Powell, Jr.—the excluded congressman who is one of the country's most prominent black politicians—in a special election. Harlem citizens generally voice anger toward the Columbia Law School undergraduate. Powell dismisses him with *"Meredith who?"* Meredith's bid will prove unsuccessful.

EUROPE

Harold Wilson

In England, Prime Minister **Harold Wilson** announces that the United Kingdom has decided to apply for European Economic Community (EEC) membership. The British pound is devalued and Wilson reassures the public that "this does not mean that the pound in your pocket or purse is worth any less." Meanwhile, the Conservatives win the Greater London Council elections.

West Berlin protests against the arrival of the **Shah of Iran** turn violent, resulting in one death.

Nicolae Ceauçescu becomes the Chairman of the Romanian State Council, effectively assuming the dictatorship of Romania.

An unstable political climate in Greece leads to an April 21 bloodless military coup which forces **King Constantine II** to flee. The new U.S.-supported totalitarian regime, led by **George Papadopoulos**, quickly moves to suspend free elections and make strikes and demonstrations illegal.

Papadopoulos on a poster and Constantine II's Greek Royal family on a stamp

ΓΕΩΡΓΙΟΣ ΠΑΠΑΔΟΠΟ
ΕΛΛΑΣ-HELLAS ΑΡ.2.50

German Chancellor **Kurt Kiesinger** & Foreign Minister **Willie Brandt** flank French President **Charles DeGaulle** during Paris talks aimed at improving relations with Iron Curtain countries. The ultimate goal is the reunification of Germany.

Over 23 million French citizens turn out to pick a new National Assembly. Returns indicate that President **Charles DeGaulle**'s coalition wins with 40% of the total vote. Frenchmen heed his call for an assembly that will support his policies stressing stability at home, first, and foreign politics, second. At right, DeGaulle emerges from the voting booth.

ANGRY CHINESE BATTLE WITH POLICE outside Red China's diplomatic office in London.

Brandishing baseball bats, iron bars and axes, the group charges the bobbies after an argument about moving a police car. Officers defend themselves with their wooden truncheons.

The clash follows a week of heavy police guard outside the delegation, after the sacking and burning of the British office outside Peking one week earlier. Mutual travel bans exist in London and Peking.

Injured are three police, three Chinese and a cameraman, none too seriously. Journalists who attempt to interview the embassy's occupants are met with a torrent of propaganda.

The increasing antagonism between the UK and Red China is in evidence again in October when British troops and Chinese demonstrators clash on the border of China and Hong Kong.

CHINA

China sends three People's Liberation Army divisions to Tibet.

The Chinese government announces that it has ordered the army to help in the spring seeding.

The People's Republic of China tests its first hydrogen bomb.

The Soviet Union announces that it has placed troops near the Chinese border. Mass demonstrations before its Peking embassy cause the Soviets to lodge a protest. The Chinese government responds that it can no longer guarantee the safety of Soviet diplomats outside the Soviet embassy grounds.

USSR

President **Lyndon Johnson**, left, meets with Soviet Premier **Aleksei Kosygin**, right, at Glassboro State College in New Jersey for the three-day Glassboro Summit Conference.

Kosygin is received by the Queen during an eight-day visit to the UK.

Moscow forbids its satellite states to form diplomatic relations with West Germany.

How does Delmont 88 deliver so many fine-car features at such a modest price?

Just beautifully.

Building cars that deliver the goods—and the goodies—comes second nature with Oldsmobile. As evidence the new Delmont 88. Toronado-inspired from stem to stern. Rocket-powered in two V-8 versions, 330 and 425 cubic inches. Proved Olds 88 chassis, brakes and suspension. A whole host of safety features, all standard. And, if you wish, such Olds engineering advancements as Climatic Combustion Control, UHV Transistorized Ignition System, front disc brakes—to name only a few. Frankly, you'd never expect a car that offers as much as Delmont 88 to carry such a modest price. But there it is, in writing, right on the sticker.

 OBEY LAWS DRIVE SAFELY — Olds thinks of your safety, too, with the GM-developed energy-absorbing steering column that can compress on severe impact up to 8¼ inches; with four-way hazard warning flasher; outside rearview mirror; dual master cylinder brake system, plus many other safety features—all standard.

Engineered for excitement ... Toronado-style!

'67 OLDSMOBILE

70

MIDDLE EAST

The Six Day War

(l to r) Israeli Generals Uzi Narkis, Moshe Dayan (Defense Minister), Yitzchak Rabin (Chief of Staff) entering Jerusalem after its capture from Jordan.

Weeks of escalating tensions between Israel, Egypt and Syria reach the boiling point when Egyptian President **Gamal Abdel-Nasser** demands the withdrawal of UN peacekeeping forces on the Egypt-Israeli border, then closes the Straits of Tiran, blockading Israel's southern port of Eilat. Jordan joins the Egyptian-Syrian military alliance, placing its troops under Egyptian command—an example followed by other Arab countries including Kuwait and Iraq.

With Arab troops arrayed along its length and invasion imminent, Israel calls up reserve forces while General **Moshe Dayan** is appointed Minister of Defense. Following the failure of last minute peace efforts by the United States, Israel launches a preemptive strike on June 5th,

Nasser

attacking Egypt in the Sinai, Syria in the Golan Heights and Jordan east of Jerusalem. Israel effectively destroys the air forces of the participating Arab states, then deploys armored divisions, winning victory in quick and dramatic fashion by

Israeli armor in the Sinai

June 10 with the Israelis occupying the West Bank, Gaza Strip, the Sinai peninsula and the Golan Heights.

On June 12 cease-fire parameters are set by UN observers and on August 1, Israel formally annexes East Jerusalem.

Iran

Mossadegh

Dr. Mohammed Mossadegh, former prime minister of Iran, dies while under house arrest. In 1953 America's Central Intelligence Agency, in concert with the British government, instituted *Project Ajax* to overthrow the democratically elected government of the popular nationalist Mossadegh and solidify the power of **Mohammad Reza Pahlavi**, the monarchal Shah of Iran, ensuring western access to Iran's rich oil reserves.

AFRICA

Moise Tshombe, the exiled ex-Prime Minister of the Democratic Republic of the **CONGO**, is sentenced to death in absentia. In June, his plane is hijacked to Algeria where he is jailed.

Congo's President **Mobutu** puts down a coup engineered by Belgian mercenary commander **Jean Schramme** and launches an offensive against the border town Bukavu, a mercenary stronghold.

Mobutu

The eastern Nigerian state **BIAFRA** secedes, declaring its independence. **NIGERIA** initially responds with an economic blockade, then sends military forces to invade, beginning the Biafran War.

A military coup takes place in **SIERRA LEONE**.

The **RHODESIAN** Parliament passes pro-Apartheid laws.

Rhodesian Prime Minister Ian Smith

INDONESIA

Following 2 years of violence in which an estimated half million Indonesians were killed by soldiers, police and vigilantes, President **Sukarno** is stripped of his title and placed under house arrest by Indonesia's provisional parliament on March 12, 1967. Army general **Suharto**, whose military spearheaded the violence with covert U.S. backing, assumes the presidency.

Sukarno

Suharto

The **AUSTRALIAN REFERENDUM** passes with an overwhelming 90% support, allowing the Government of Australia to make special laws for the benefit of indigenous Australians (Aborigines).

INDIA

A peasant uprising in the town of Naxalbari begins the Naxalite Guerrilla War, the Marxist/Maoist rebellion born out of the Sino-Soviet split in the Indian communist movement.

Dr. Zakir Hussain is the first Muslim president of India.

Charu Majumdar and Kanu Sanyal, Naxalite movement leaders.

In the **PHILIPPINES**, the province of Davao is split into three: Davao del Norte, Davao del Sur, and Davao Oriental.

LATIN AMERICA

General **Anastasio Somoza Debayle** becomes president of **NICARAGUA** shortly before the death of his brother, Luis Somoza Debayle, and quickly establishes a harshly repressive military dictatorship.

A group of young radicals who advocate armed struggle are expelled from the Moscow-loyal Nicaraguan Socialist Party (PSN). The group goes on to found the Socialist Workers Party (POS).

Humberto Castelo Branco finishes his term as president of **BRAZIL** and dies in a plane crash shortly thereafter.

Fidel Castro announces that all intellectual property belongs to all people and that **CUBA** intends to translate and publish technical literature without compensation.

The island nation **DOMINICA** gains independence from the United Kingdom

Donald Sangster becomes the new Prime Minister of JAMAICA, succeeding Alexander Bustamante.

Following a strike action in MEXICO which ends in shooting and deaths, rural schoolteacher Lucio Cabañas flees to the mountains and begins a guerrilla campaign in Atoyac de Alvarez, west of Acapulco in the state of Guerrero. He aims to defeat the government of the rich and install a new regime with social reform for the country's poor.

Passings

CLEMENT ATTLEE (74), former Prime Minister of the United Kingdom.

Argentinean Ernesto Guevara de la Serna, popularly known as **CHE GUEVARA** (39), is captured and summarily executed by Bolivian army troops. The Marxist revolutionary became involved in Guatamala's social movement and later helped Castro seize power in Cuba, where he took a post in the new government. He left Cuba in 1965 to foment revolution in various parts of the world. Legend has it that his last words were "Shoot, coward. You're only going to kill a man."

Che and Cuba's Fidel Castro

America will need seven times as much power by the year 2000. We'll be ready for that, and more.

This forecast means we'll have to build <u>seven times</u> the equivalent of all we've built since 1882 in the next 33 years! Through sound business planning, and financing in the open money market, we'll help good things happen for customers, employees, supporting businesses and investors while we increase our country's electric power supply.

The electric company people... the folks at your Investor-Owned Electric Light and Power Companies*

*For names of sponsoring companies, write to Power Companies, 1271 Avenue of the Americas, New York, N.Y. 10020.

People

In New York, a royal reception greets Britain's top model, the 17-year old cockney girl whose professional name is

TWIGGY

Her real name is **Leslie Hornby** and she's accompanied by boyfriend/manager, **Justin de Villeneuve** (former hairdresser Nigel Davies), who fields most of the reporter's questions.

Twiggy stands 5 foot 6 inches, weighs 91 pounds and sports measurements 31-22-32. She says her fondest wish while in the States is to visit Disneyland and meet boxer Muhammad Ali.

The Elusive Mr. K

A Moscow street is the scene for a rare public appearance by former Soviet Premier **Nikita Khrushchev**, who chats with a journalist while on his way to cast his vote for the man who helped oust him, Premier Kosygin. It's the first time in nine months that Mr. K walks among the people he once ruled and they show their affection.

U Thant Goes Home Again

In Rangoon, Burma, United Nations Secretary-General **U Thant** hosts a ceremonial meal for Bhuddist monks during his first visit home in three years. After meetings with North Vietnamese representatives, Thant predicts that, unless the United States unconditionally halts bombing the North, the war could be prolonged and bloody.

Rock & Roll Babylon

Beatle JOHN LENNON commissions a psychedelic paint job from a team of Dutch artists for his 1965 Rolls-Royce Phantom V. An outraged London woman attacks the car with an umbrella, shouting "You swine! How dare you do this to a Rolls-Royce!"

Rolling Stones Mick Jagger, Keith Richards, Brian Jones

Jim Morrison

The British Sunday tabloid *News of the World* publishes a series entitled "Pop Stars and Drugs—Facts that Will Shock You," in which drug abuse is alleged against a number of popular rock musicians. A feud is ignited when **Rolling Stones** singer **Mick Jagger**—whom the article claims is a user of benzedrine and hashish—launches a defamation lawsuit against the paper. A tip from *News Of The World* reporters leads to a police raid on Stones' guitarist **Keith Richards**' Sussex home and the arrest of Richards and Jagger, among others. Richards is charged and stands trial for allowing drug use in his home and is sentenced to a year's imprisonment. Jagger is charged with possessing amphetamine without a doctor's prescription and receives a four month sentence. Both convictions are later overturned on appeal.

DOING SULLIVAN

In January, the **Rolling Stones** appear on the The **Ed Sullivan** TV show and at Sullivan's request, change the lyrics of *Let's Spend the Night Together* to "let's spend some time together."

Not quite as accomodating for their September Sullivan performance, **The Doors** ignore the warning of CBS censors when **Jim Morrison** sings intact the line, "Girl we couldn't get much *higher*" from their hit song, *Light My Fire*. Sullivan is so angry he refuses to shake hands with the group. An exultant Morrison reputedly crows "We just *did* the Sullivan show."

Morrison courts controversy again in December when he maligns police from the stage during a Connecticut concert and is arrested—charged with disturbing the peace and resisting arrest.

Two members of the rock group MOBY GRAPE are arrested for contributing to the delinquency of minors.

PLAY FOR PAY

The Animals, famous for hits like *San Franciscan Nights* and *House of the Rising Sun*, refuse to perform in Ontario unless they are paid in advance. The audience reacts violently and the night ends with $5,000 worth of damage to the auditorium.

Outside the District Court building in the nation's capitol, Teamsters boss James R.

HOFFA SURRENDERS

to U.S. Marshals to begin serving an 8-year prison term for tampering with a grand jury witness while attempting to secure an acquittal on charges of "shaking down" a trucking company.

With his raincoat covering handcuffs, Hoffa arrives at the federal prison in Lewisburg, Pennsylvania. He says his attorneys will continue his fight while he's in jail. Parole is possible in 32 months. At $100,000 annually, Hoffa is the nation's highest-paid prisoner.

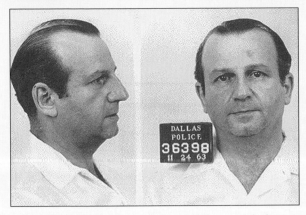

JACK RUBY (born Jacob Leon Rubenstein) dies at age 56 of a pulmonary embolism. Ruby murdered Lee Harvey Oswald on November 24, 1963, two days after Oswald's arrest for the assassination of President John F. Kennedy. In 1966, the appellate court agreed with Ruby's lawyers that his motion for change of venue should have been granted before the first trial ever began. His conviction and death sentence are overturned, but before a new trial can take place, Ruby is admitted to Dallas' Parkland Hospital with pneumonia and succumbs.

Pioneering British record producer **JOE MEEK** kills his landlady and himself with a shotgun. Meek, famous for producing the **Tornados** hit *Telstar*—the first record by a British act to hit #1 in the U.S. charts—was obsessed with **Buddy Holly** and other dead musicians. He suffered bouts of paranoia, drug use and depression. His violent rampage occurs on February 3, the eighth anniversary of Buddy Holly's death.

 In Munich, the trial of **WILHELM HARSTER** gets underway. Harster led the German security police during the occupation of the Netherlands and stands complicit in the murder of over 82,000 Jews, including **Anne Frank**. He is sentenced to 15 years in prison.

SERIAL KILLERS

Speck and a police rendering

"Boston Strangler" ALBERT DeSALVO confesses to the sexual assault and murder of 13 women from 1962 to 1964. With no evidence to substansiate his confession, he is convicted of earlier unrelated crimes and sentenced to life in prison, where he is murdered six years later.

Mass murderer RICHARD SPECK is sentenced to death for the killing of eight student nurses from South Chicago Community Hospital the previous year. Speck held the women hostage for hours, beating and raping them before finally stabbing them to death. He avoids the electric chair when the Supreme Court outlaws capital punishment the following year, and is resentenced to 50 to 100 years in prison.

In July, the mutilated, decomposing body of Michigan University student Mary Fleszar is discovered, the first in a string of coed murders continuing through 1969. "**Michigan Murderer**" JOHN NORMAN COLLINS will eventually be charged with the crimes and sentenced to life in prison without parole.

MUHAMMAD ALI's biggest fight of the year comes when he refuses to serve in the U.S. army and fight in the Vietnam War. Claiming status as a conscientious objector, Ali declares, "War is against the teachings of the Holy Koran. I'm not trying to dodge the draft. We are supposed to take part in no wars unless declared by Allah or The Messenger. We don't take part in Christian wars or wars of any unbelievers. I ain't got no quarrel with those Viet Cong." The World Boxing Association strips Ali of his championship belt and boxing license, calling him "a very poor example for the young people of the world." An all-white Houston jury eventually finds Ali guilty of draft evasion, and he is sentenced to five years in prison and a $10,000 fine. The sentence is overturned on appeal four years later by a unanimous Supreme Court decision.

Spock, l, and Ginsberg

Benjamin Spock, famous pediatrician and author of *Baby and Child Care*, and Beat poet **Allen Ginsberg** are arrested while protesting the war in Vietnam.

Father **Philip Berrigan** and his brother, Father **Daniel Berrigan** pour animal blood onto files in a Baltimore Selective Service Office in protest of the war. Philip is sentenced to 9 years in prison.

French journalist **Régis Debray** is convicted of aiding **Che Guevara**'s guerilla group. Sentenced to 30 years in jail in Bolivia, he is freed in 1970 following an international clemency campaign.

Debray, r, with his Bolivian captors.

Wilson

Singer **Jackie Wilson** and his friend, drummer **Jimmy Smith**, are arrested on morals charges when they are found in a South Carolina motel with two 24-year-old white women. To rehabilitate his public reputation, Wilson marries longtime girlfriend **Harlean Harris**. The penalty against the musicians is reduced to a fine of several hundred dollars.

Mildred Jeter, a black woman, and white bricklayer **Richard Loving** receive suspended one-year jail sentences for violating Virginia's ban on interracial marriage. The sentencing judge states "Almighty God created the races white, black, yellow, malay, and red, and he placed them on separate continents... The fact that he separated the races shows that he did not intend for the races to mix."

Democratic Senator **Thomas J. Dodd** is censured by the Senate for personal use of campaign funds, and **Robert "Bobby" Baker**, former secretary to the Senate Democrats, is sentenced to 1-3 years for conspiracy and tax evasion.

British Prime Minister **Harold Wilson** sues the pop group **The Move** for libel when the band's manager publishes a promotional postcard with a cartoon caricature of Wilson in bed with his female assistant. Wilson wins the case, and all royalties from the The Move's hit song *Flowers In The Rain* are assigned in perpetuity to a charity of Wilson's choice.

The Move

Ballet stars Dame **Margot Fonteyn** and **Rudolf Nureyev**, currently appearing in *Romeo and Juliet*, create a stir when they are held overnight in a police station after being arrested in a raid in San Francisco's Haight-Ashbury district.

When actress and activist **Melina Mercouri**'s Greek citizenship is revoked, she declares, "I was born Greek and I will die Greek. Mr. [Interior Minister Stylianos] Pattakos was born a dictator and he will die as a dictator." Mercouri makes her home in France for the duration of the dictatorship in Greece.

During an official state visit to Montreal, Canada, French President **Charles de Gaulle** declares to a crowd of over 100,000: "Vive le Québec libre!" (Long live free Quebec!) Although this delights many Quebec citizens, the Canadian government and English Canadians are angered.

New Orleans District Attorney **Jim Garrison** avers that the assassination of **John F. Kennedy** was planned in New Orleans, that the Warren Commission report is a coverup and that he is going to get to the bottom of it. There are those, he says in a *Playboy* magazine interview, who "don't want the truth about Kennedy's assassination to become known."

"There was a plan in operation in the city of New Orleans, which had entirely different objectives than the killing of the President. That was the last thing on the minds of the people that caused this plan to begin. Lee Harvey Oswald was a part, assigned a role, essentially as decoy."

"...as a result of the operation, which was working here in the summer of 1963, a spinoff occurred, an unexpected change of direction occurred, which, in the fall of 1963, resulted in that lethal apparatus being turned against President Kennedy. And that's what happened, and that's the first time I've ever said it publicly."

—from an NBC News interview

Josef Stalin's daughter **Svetlana Alliluyeva** defects to the United States. Upon her arrival, she holds a press conference denouncing her father's regime and the Soviet government. Due to the publicity generated by her high-profile defection, the Soviet Union demands and receives an assurance from the United States that any future defectors will be debriefed by Soviet officials before being granted asylum.

Stalin with daughter Svetlana in 1935.

Acapulco Affair

In Acapulco, a lavish dinner party attracts a variety of celebrities including first daughter **Lynda Bird Johnson** and her actor friend **George Hamilton** (above). Film stars **Dolores del Rio** (with husband, top right) and **John Wayne** (right) also enjoy the festivities. A request to have press barred from the party was refused.

While they spend the gay evening as almost constant dancing partners, Linda and George refuse to comment on speculation about a future wedding, even though *Modern Screen* magazine reports Hamilton's declaration of love for Lynda Bird. Nevertheless, her affair with Hamilton fizzles and Lynda Bird winds up marrying Marine Captain **Charles S. Robb** some months later in a splendid ceremony in the East Room of the White House.

Weddings

ELVIS PRESLEY (32) marries **PRISCILLA ANNE BEAULIEU** (21) at the Aladdin hotel in Las Vegas. The *Las Vegas Sun* reports "Following the ceremony, attended by a few relatives and close friends, an elaborate banquet was held just below the hotel's casino. An estimated 100 guests dined on ham, eggs, Southern fried chicken, Oysters Rockefeller, roast suckling pig, poached and candied salmon, lobster, Eggs Minnette, and champagne."

Leslie Ann Warren *and* Jon Peters

Liza Minelli *and* Peter Allen

Sharon Lee Perry *and* John D. Rockefeller

Raquel Welch *and* Patrick Curtis

Ann-Margret *and* Roger Smith

Eddie Fisher *and* Connie Stevens (his 3rd wife)

Jane Fonda *and* Roger Vadim

Margrethe, heir apparent to the throne of Denmark, marries French **Count Henri de Laborde de Monpezat.**

Julie Nixon gets engaged to **David Eisenhower**; both are only 19 years old.

DIVORCES

Jon Voight *and* **Lauri Peters**

Tony Curtis *and* **Christine Kaufmann**

Sandra Dee *and* **Bobby Darin**

Sheila McRae *and* **Gordon McRae**

ZsaZsa Gabor *and* **Joseph Cosden**

Pete Candoli *and* **Betty Hutton**

Mickey Rooney *and* **Marge Lane**

"Always get married in the morning. That way if it doesn't work out, you haven't wasted the whole day."
—Mickey Rooney

When singer and actress **Barbra Streisand** forgets the words to several songs during a concert in New York's Central Park, she picks up a major case of stage fright and does not sing in public again until 1994 during her comeback tour.

• • •

Singer **Tammi Terrell** faints in **Marvin Gaye**'s arms during a performance. She will be diagnosed with a brain tumor.

• • •

FROM THE MOUTHS OF BABES...

Four-year-old **David Belote** of Virginia impresses President Johnson and the guides on his White House tour when he recites the names of all the U.S. Presidents—in order!

• • •

FROZEN FOR THE FUTURE

Psychology professor **Dr. James Bedford**, 73, is the first person cryonically preserved (frozen) with the intent of future resuscitation.

ALL GROWN UP

Former child movie star **SHIRLEY TEMPLE BLACK** announces her candidacy for congress to fill a California vacancy left by the death of J. Arthur Younger. She says she'll run as a Republican Independent and her announcement includes a strong attack on the Johnson administration.

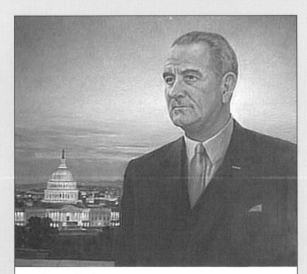

In the 30s, the curly-haired, dimpled Shirley Temple captured the hearts of America and the world in over 40 charming films. Today, the 39-year old mother of 3 seeks to join two other former stars in politics—Governor Ronald Reagan and Senator George Murphy—but her election bid will ultimately fail.

LBJ is *Time* Magazine's Person of the Year for the second time. The first was in 1964.

Gallup reports that Americans choose President **Dwight D. Eisenhower** as the man they most admire this year. **Lyndon Johnson** takes the number two spot, followed by **Reverend Billy Graham**, **Robert F. Kennedy**, **Pope Paul VI**, **Senator Everett M. Dirksen**, **Richard M. Nixon**, **George C. Wallace**, and **Ronald Reagan**.

Harold Holt, Australian Prime Minister, disappears while swimming at a beach 60 kilometers from Melbourne, his body apparently swept out to sea.

Benjamin Netanyahu, future Prime Minister of Israel from 1996 to 1999, joins the Israeli Army.

LBJ calls his portrait, painted by Peter Hurd, "the ugliest thing I ever saw."

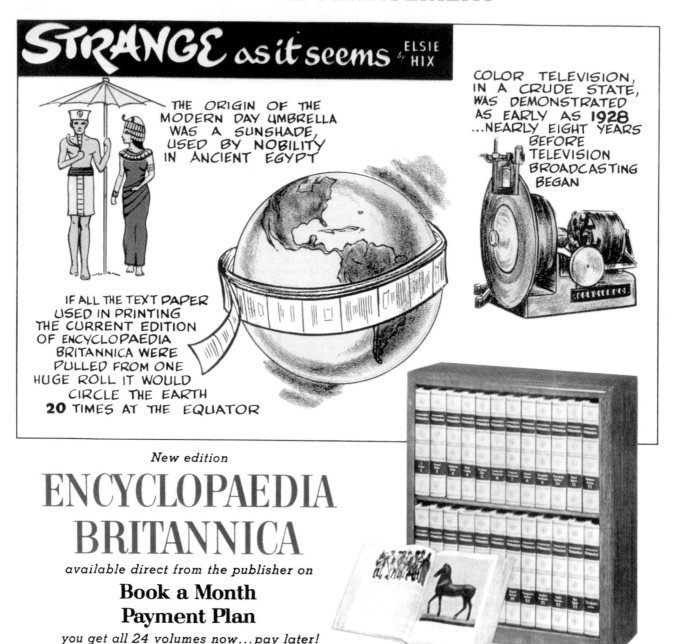

STRANGE *as it seems* by ELSIE HIX

THE ORIGIN OF THE MODERN DAY UMBRELLA WAS A SUNSHADE, USED BY NOBILITY IN ANCIENT EGYPT

COLOR TELEVISION, IN A CRUDE STATE, WAS DEMONSTRATED AS EARLY AS 1928 ...NEARLY EIGHT YEARS BEFORE TELEVISION BROADCASTING BEGAN

IF ALL THE TEXT PAPER USED IN PRINTING THE CURRENT EDITION OF ENCYCLOPAEDIA BRITANNICA WERE PULLED FROM ONE HUGE ROLL IT WOULD CIRCLE THE EARTH **20** TIMES AT THE EQUATOR

New edition

ENCYCLOPAEDIA BRITANNICA

available direct from the publisher on

Book a Month Payment Plan

you get all 24 volumes now...pay later!

The latest edition of Britannica—the greatest treasury of knowledge ever published—is the greatest in our almost 200-year publishing history. An *enormous printing* materially reduces our costs and under a remarkable direct-from-the-publisher plan, we pass these benefits on to you. All 24 handsome volumes of this world-renowned reference library will be delivered to your home NOW *direct from the publisher.* You pay later at a cost so low it is as easy as buying a book a month!

Equivalent to a library of 1,000 books

Encyclopaedia Britannica is the most valuable gift you can give yourself and your family—the priceless gift of knowledge. Information on every subject significant to mankind is contained in its new edition. It is equivalent to a library of 1,000 books, bringing you the knowledge and authority of world-recognized leaders in every field.

Just think of a subject—and you'll find it in Encyclopaedia Britannica—whether it is infor-

mation on the rules of a sport, the background of a religion, how to build a brick arch in a fireplace, or the science of launching a guided missile.

The new Britannica almost "televises" information to you, with over 22,000 magnificent photographs, maps and drawings. In every respect, Britannica is the largest and most complete reference set published in America, containing more than 28,000 pages and over 36,000,000 words.

Symbol of a good home

Encyclopaedia Britannica cannot help but have a lasting effect on you as well as on the growth and development of your children in school and in later life. Benjamin Franklin said, "An investment in knowledge pays the best interest," and Britannica gives you the accumulated knowledge of the world in clear, easy-to-read language and superb illustrations. It is essential in every home where education is valued and respected.

Preview Booklet Offered FREE

Simply fill in and mail the attached card today,

and we will send you ... without cost or obligation ... a copy of our beautiful new booklet which contains an exciting preview of the latest edition of Encyclopaedia Britannica. Mail no money. It's yours, absolutely free! However, to avoid disappointment, please mail the attached card today before it slips your mind.

Mail the attached card now for FREE BOOKLET

Just tear out attached card, fill in and mail for your free Preview Booklet of the new edition of Encyclopaedia Britannica. Or write to Encyclopaedia Britannica, Dept. 550-V, 425 North Michigan Ave., Chicago, Illinois 60611.

Watch National Geographic's "Alaska!" brought to you by Encyclopaedia Britannica, in color on CBS-TV at 7:30 p.m. (E.S.T.) Tuesday, February 7.

Human Interest

On the Chinese calendar, 1967 is the *Year of the Ram* (or Sheep or Goat). According to Chinese astrology, those born in the year of the ram tend to be charming, amiable, and sympathetic, always looking for the best in others and themselves. They live in the present, and are the most creative and expressive of all the signs in the Chinese Zodiac.

Famous folks who fall under the sign of the ram include: **Michelangelo, Mel Gibson, Chow Yun Fat, Jimmy Smits, Kurt Cobain, John Kerry, Joni Mitchell, Bill Gates, George Harrison, Bruce Willis** and **Dennis Wilson.**

JUST THE FACTS

President **Lyndon B. Johnson**

Vice President **Hubert H. Humphrey**

US Population 👪 **198,712,056**

US Life Expectancy 🕐 **70.5 years**

US Violent Crime Rate **29.9 per 1,000**

US Property Crime Rate 🏠 **27.4 per 1,000**

US Homicide Rate **6.8 per 100,000**

World Population **3.485 billion**

"I was suddenly aware of this whole scene. Something was going on . . . I went to Haight-Ashbury for about two months. The Summer of Love . . . I felt I had fallen into some Utopia whose millennium had arrived. I was heedless of the future, and my past as well."

— a Los Angeles teenager

HUMAN BE-IN KICKS OFF *SUMMER of LOVE*

In January, more than 20,000 people, responding to an announcement on the cover of the first issue of the *San Francisco Oracle*, flock to "a gathering of the tribes for a human be-in" in San Francisco's Golden Gate Park. Dressed in a manner which they believe expressess their true 'inner selves,' young people watch poet **Allen Ginsberg** open the festivities with a chanted hindu blessing, followed by local rock acts **The Grateful Dead**, **Jefferson Airplane** and **Quicksilver Messenger Service**. Other counterculture personalities present amid the wafting pot and incense vapors include **Richard Alpert** (Ram Dass), poet **Gary Snyder**, comedian **Dick Gregory** and activist **Jerry Rubin**. The **Hells Angels** motorcycle gang provide security and round up lost children.

Abbie Hoffman

HIPPIES reject traditional values in favor of an anti-establishment outlook. Sporting long hair, brightly colored clothes and occasionally painted faces, they opt for illicit drugs, uninhibited sex and group habitation.

THE DIGGERS, a group of artists and activists, preach the "free doctrine," scavenging food, clothing, furniture and other items and giving them away at Golden Gate Park and their Free Store. Meanwhile, **Abbie Hoffman** opens his own Free Store in New York as the Summer of Love culture moves across the country.

The **HAIGHT-ASHBURY** Free Medical Clinic is created by **Dr. David Smith** who believes that "health care is a right, not a privilege."

By early October, the Summer of Love is dying, and many hippies head out to rural communities. Community members hold a mock funeral, carrying a fake dead hippie through San Francisco's streets and staging a sad burial.

The UNDERGROUND PRESS

Building on the success of the *Los Angeles Free Press*, alternative newspapers like *The Great Speckled Bird*, *The East Village Other*, *Vortex*, *The Seed*, *Kudzu* and others respond to the emerging hippie culture, boasting a combined circulation of several million.

The Los Angeles Advocate, the first national gay and lesbian news magazine, hits the stands. Founded by gay rights activists Dick Michaels and Bill Rand after a 1966 raid on a Los Angeles gay bar, it will later become known simply as *The Advocate*.

Zap Comix number 0 depicts a naked man being zapped on its cover. Created by San Francisco cartoonist Robert Crumb, it features sex, drugs, profanity, pokes fun at Jesus and quickly becomes a cult classic.

CHARLES BUKOWSKI's column *Notes of a Dirty Old Man* is popular in the underground newspaper *OPEN CITY*. One of his early pieces satirizes Hemingway and is titled "An Old Drunk who Ran Out of Luck."

At a New Year's Eve party, **Abbie Hoffman**, **Jerry Rubin**, **Paul Krassner**, **Dick Gregory** and others call themselves "Yippies" and plan to attend the Democratic Convention the following year.

In February, 2,500 members of **Women's Strike for Peace**, including many mothers and relatives of soldiers, march on the Pentagon and demand to meet with Secretary of Defense Robert McNamara.

In October, recruiters from **Dow Chemical**, the manufacturers of the jellied incendiary napalm, are driven away by student protestors at the University of Wisconsin. Protestors chant "Dow burns babies!" A Wisconsin state assemblyman says of the protestors, "Shoot them if necessary. I would… it's insurrection."

THE DRAFT

In March, the Presidential Selective Service Commission calls for a lottery system drafting 19-year olds first for the military.

Over 900 American men are convicted of violations of U.S. draft laws.

"STOP THE DRAFT WEEK" hits the U.S. in mid-October. Students from the San Francisco Bay area put their bodies in front of buses unloading potential recruits at the Oakland induction center. Women carry signs reading, *Women Say Yes to Men who Say No*. The activity begins peacefully, but by the second day, police in riot gear clash with protestors. Men across the country burn their draft cards, and the week ends with 50,000 marching on the Pentagon. In New Haven, Connecticut, 30 of 300 protestors are arrested when they shout "Hell, no! We won't go!" in front of the induction center.

RESIST

OCTOBER 16

Discover Hawaii 1967
...in the world's biggest, newest jet – the Super DC-8

Starting this month, United puts new luxury into the skies between California and Hawaii. The luxury of flying in the world's newest, roomiest jet . . . the luxury of 2 extra stewardesses serving up United's famous "Extra Care." Add the exotic foods and beverages, six channel stereo, widescreen color movies, and—well, it's like being in Hawaii 5 hours ahead of time! Join us? United's the only airline flying the "Big New Ones" to Hawaii and we're looking forward to welcoming you aboard.

"It's like one big happy Luau!"

fly the friendly skies of United.

Films by Inflight Motion Pictures

Human Interest

A large mural in Chicago, known as the WALL OF RESPECT, depicts images of accomplished African-Americans such as Marcus Garvey, H. Rap Brown, Stokely Carmichael, Muhammad Ali, Sarah Vaughn and John Coltrane.

New York's chapter of NOW (National Organization for Women) pickets The *New York Times* in protest of the paper's sex-segregated job listings.

Democratic Senator **Eugene McCarthy** introduces the Equal Rights Amendment.

Educator **Jonathan Kozol**'s book *Death At An Early Age*, details the apalling conditions in Boston's elementary schools in the mainly black Roxbury district. Boston's mayoral race draws attention when **Louise Day Hicks**, an opponent of school integration, takes 47% of the vote, losing to **Kevin H. White** by 11,000 votes.

Congress passes the Age Discrimination Act, which prohibits employment discrimination toward Americans 40 and older.

LBJ asks Congress for Social Security hikes.

Colorado becomes the first state to liberalize abortion laws, okaying legal abortion for pregnancies resulting from rape, incest or other specific conditions.

The federal government eliminates draft deferments for anyone violating the draft laws or attempting to interfere with recruitment.

Actress **Betty Furness** is named Special Assistant for Consumer Affairs to President Johnson. She becomes a lightning rod for criticism when she admits she has "not been in a supermarket in six years" and that her housekeeper knows more about prices than she does.

The President's Commission on Law Enforcement reports that one-third of Americans have firearms and feel unsafe walking outside at night.

The House of Representatives makes it a federal offense to cross a state line in order to incite a riot.

Sixty nations sign a United Nations treaty calling for peaceful uses of outer space.

The crew of the U.S. aircraft carrier *Franklin D. Roosevelt* is confined to ship in Cape Town, South Africa—it is felt that its racially diverse company will not mix well with the town's Apartheid policy.

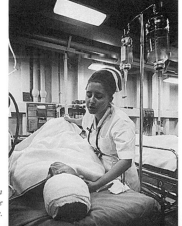

Approximately 80% of the 7,500 women serving in Vietnam work in the nurse corps, and after the war, hundreds suffer from post-traumatic stress disorder.

Nurse with post-op patient in the intensive care ward of the hospital ship USS Repose.

POPE PAUL VI publishes his *Encyclical Populorum Progressio* (On the Development of Peoples), wherein he argues:

"Extreme disparity between nations in economic, social and educational levels provokes jealousy and discord, often putting peace in jeopardy…. When we fight poverty and oppose the unfair conditions of the present, we are not just promoting human well-being; we are also furthering man's spiritual and moral development, and hence we are benefiting the whole human race."

A Church in downtown Madrid marks
A New Day in Spanish Religious History

For the first time, Catholics and Jews pray together. Jewish leader **Max Mazin** speaks at the service celebrating the passage of a law giving non-Catholics religious freedom in Spain and the forthcoming repeal of the edict of expulsion—first issued against Spanish Jews in 1492 by Ferdinand and Isabella.

Mazin

Alvarez

Father Alvarez shares the pulpit, pointing out the kinship of Catholic prayers and Jewish psalms. The law is hailed as a harvest from the seed which **Pope John XXIII** planted in the conscience of mankind.

Amazing Animals

A Star is Born

The world's first known white gorilla is found in Africa's Equatorial Guinea, still clinging to the back of its dead mother. The 19 ¹/₂ pound albino baby is shipped to the home of Roman Luera Carbo, Chief Veterinarian of the Barcelona zoo. Dubbed "Snowflake," he becomes the zoo's irresistible attraction and an international star.

NO MOTHER-OF-THE-YEAR AWARD FOR YOU!

ROSIE, a whooping crane at the San Antonio, Texas zoo lays two eggs that hatch in July. Rosie accidentally sits on the first hatchling, crushing it to death. When the second chick hatches, officials take it away to save its life.

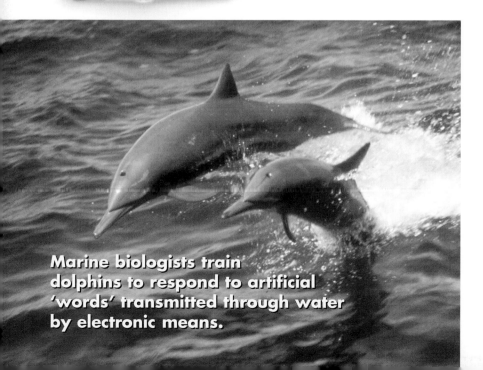

Marine biologists train dolphins to respond to artificial 'words' transmitted through water by electronic means.

Two 100,000,000-year old ants preserved in amber are identified, almost doubling the known time period of the ants' ancestry.

RECORD BREAKERS

Test pilot **Pete Knight** establishes an unofficial world fixed-wing speed record of Mach 6.7 in an X-15 research aircraft.

Daredevil **Evel Knievel** jumps his motorcycle over 16 cars in a row at the Ascot Speedway in Gardena, California.

WHAT A FIND!

Ernestine Ramoboa finds the world's 7th largest diamond (601.25 carats) while sifting through gravel in Lesotho, Africa. Jeweler Harry Winston pays $302,400 for the stone, and the Ramoboas receive over $150,000 for themselves.

Robert Alcock beats 23 women to win the title of Champion Knitter of King's Lynn, England. Alcock owes his knitting expertise to the fact that he uses the craft to treat his rheumatism.

• • •

Harvey M. Friedman is the youngest person ever to receive a doctor's degree from M.I.T. when he gets his Ph.D. in math just a few days shy of his 19th birthday.

• • •

Creme Puff, born in Austin, Texas in 1967 is the oldest living cat and still going strong as of her 38th birthday on August 3rd, 2005.

Briton **Rodney Sumpter** sets a world record for distance surfing: 9.6 km.

• • •

Some impressive "squidging" is on display when a 4-pot relay world record is set in Tiddlywinks: 44 winks in the requisite 3 minutes.

RECORD-SETTING CONSTRUCTION PROJECTS

Lake Point Tower

The 70-story Lake Point Tower in Chicago measures 645 feet tall, and is the world's tallest reinforced concrete structure.

Cowlitz River Bridge becomes the longest concrete arch in the U.S. in December, crossing Mayfield Lake near Mossyrick, Washington.

The world's longest orthotropic bridge, the San Mateo-Hayward Bridge across San Francisco Bay, opens in October at a cost of $70,000,000.

Venezuela's Angostura Bridge over the Orinoco River opens six months early; it is the longest clear suspension bridge in South America.

Angostura Bridge

THE OSTANKINO TOWER IN MOSCOW IS COMPLETED, BECOMING THE TALLEST FREE-STANDING STRUCTURE IN THE WORLD AT 1,772 FEET.

Ostankino Tower

British ocean liner **Queen Mary** makes her last transatlantic crossing before being permanently berthed in Long Beach, California where she becomes a hotel and museum. Originally launched in 1934, Long Beach pays $3.45 million for the ship.

QUEEN MARY

Now get the
grooming action
of a hair cream
from a liquid.

and that's not all.

©1967 Bristol-Myers Co.

*If you haven't been getting all you want
from a liquid hair groom, get new Score Liquid.
Gives you the great grooming action of a cream.
That's because new clear Score Liquid is made by
the men who make clear Score Hair Cream.
So you get great grooming action.
And you also get Score's famous greaseless look,
Score's famous masculine scent.*

Score® Liquid Hair Groom

Score–Three ways.™ Hair Cream. Spray Deodorant. Liquid Hair Groom.

What's New

National Pavilions
Pavillons thématiques
Theme Pavilions
Expo-Services et réalisations de l'Expo
Expo-Services and Expo Projects

Park areas
Stationnement
Parking
Stations du Métro
Métro stations

La Balade/Trailer Tra
Hovercraft
Bac/Ferry

PONT VICTORIA BRIDGE

HAVRE

expo67
FRANCE

expo67
GREAT BRITAIN

River

expo67

Numéros de renvoi au plan:*

Key to map numbers:*

115 Route Bonaventure
200 Autostade/Automotive Stadium
201 Plac
202 La B
     d'Ac
     Stop
203 Exp
205 Term
     Hav
     Hav
206 Zone
     Stad
207 Cent
     (R.C
     (C.B

stration et de la
Presse/Administration and News
Pavilion
209 Stationnement de l'Administration/
     Administration Parking
210 Musée d'Art/Art Gallery

Olympic House

231 Quai Mark Drouin/Mark Drouin Quay
232 Passage du Quai/Quay Underpass
233 Expo-Express, Station "Habitat 67"

re, Arrêt
Havre Trailer

re, Arrêt
Havre Trailer

247 La Balade Cité du Havre, Arrêt "Pa
     l'Habitat"/Cité du Havre Trailer Tra
248 Parc de l'Habitat/Habitat Park
250 Pointe du Havre/Harbour Point

expo67

More than 50 million people visit the International and Universal Exposition—the World's Fair known as Expo 67— in Montreal, Quebec, Canada. Coinciding with the Canadian Centennial, 90 pavilions representing nations, corporations and industries are featured. The U.S. display is housed in a geodesic dome designed by Buckminster Fuller.

Bienvenue À
Welcome to
expo67

New Products and Inventions

MICROWAVE COOKING ARRIVES WITH THE AMANA RADARANGE

Amana introduces the first countertop microwave oven, selling for about $500. Smaller and more affordable than its predecessors, the 115-volt **Radarange** has just two control knobs—one cooks for up to 5 minutes, the other up to 25 minutes—in addition to a start and on/off button.

The New Cars

PORS
STUTTGAR

MERCURY COUGAR:
Winner of the *Motor Trend* magazine
Car of the Year 1967

Car of the Year 1967 MERCURY COUGAR

FORD
rolls out
"European
elegance"
at popular prices.

Ford

...has a better idea

THUNDERBIRD

Cortina wins East African Safari Rally

Nairobi, Kenya. British-built Cortina GT's have just won the East African Safari Rally. The modest looking family [ca]rs, rally modified, triumphed over the 3,188-mile run often called the toughest in the world, finishing first and [secon]d over 92 others. Only 21 entries made it all the way. Four were Cortinas — a remarkable demonstration of [per]formance. Victories like the Safari are becoming a habit with this rugged performer. Cortinas [won ...] out of 27 international competitions to date, including firsts-in-class at Marlboro, Sebring, [... Pe]nsacola, a clean sweep of recent U.S. meets against other competition-modified cars.

Cortina makes new friends all over America

FOOD IN THE NEWS

BURGERS ARE HOT

McDonald's introduces its stand-alone restaurant design with indoor seating, and the first international McDonald's opens in British Columbia.

Pillsbury acquires **Burger King** • **Ralston Purina** buys **Jack in the Box** • **General Foods** purchases the **Burger Chef** chain

HOT DOGS ARE BIG

Frankfurters are the year's most popular sausage product, representing about 25% of all sausage sold in North America.

Shaken, not stirred...

Vodka surpasses gin in popularity, thanks in part to **Ian Fleming**'s secret agent James Bond, who prefers vodka to gin martinis – shaken, not stirred!

NEW
AT A STORE NEAR YOU

* Carnation **Instant Breakfast**
  "...makes milk a meal too good to miss"

* Maxwell House **Max-Pax**
  pre-measured coffee rings

* **Chef Boy-Ar-Dee Pizza**
  pizza kit-in-a-box

* General Foods' **Tost'em Pop-Ups**
  fruit-filled toaster pastries

* General Mills' **Bugles** cone-shaped chips

BREAKFAST OF CHAMPIONS

Baseball's **Bobby Richardson**, **Tim McCarver** and **Joe Horlen** and football's **Raymond Berry** all grace the cover of the **Wheatie's** Breakfast of Champions cereal box.

Miracle Whip salad dressing is introduced in England, and the **Chiquita** banana label arrives in Europe.

LOOK
Magazine

"Youth '67, get set to flip over a new crowd pleaser, chocolate fondue. What began as a publicity gimmick has taken off like a space dish."

CHOCOLATE

1967 ADVERTISEMENT

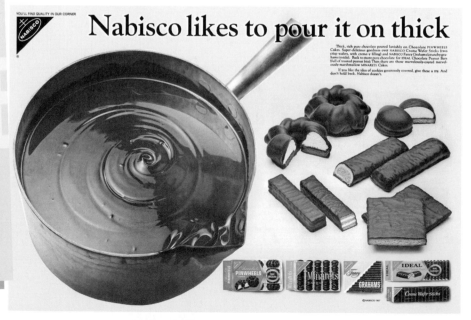

Nabisco likes to pour it on thick

FANCY YOURSELF A GOURMET?
Tips from *Betty Crocker's Hostess Cookbook*

" Betty Crocker's Extra-Special Dinner Party Starring Beef Wellington – Here is a menu that very clearly stars a spectacular entree. Dramatic, delicious Beef Wellington demands all the cook's time and talent, so everything that goes with it is as super-simplified as planning and convenience foods can make it. A smart hostessing trick!... This stunning main dish is accompanied by canned and frozen vegetables chosen to ease the preparation and to color-complement the meat. The quick-mix dessert is glamourously garnished and can be served flaming, if you like. "

BETTY SUGGESTS THIS SAMPLE MENU

• Start with canned beef consomme, tomato juice and Daisy's snack crackers.

• Move on to your spinach-apple salad with mayonnaise-frozen orange juice dressing.

• Add your main course – tenderloin of Beef Wellington, canned potatoes parmesan, frozen carrot nuggets with brown sugar, and frozen green peas and onions with butter sauce.

• Finish up with lemon cake with lemon frosting (from mix), garnished with chopped green grapes and pistachios (optional flaming sugar cubes on top).

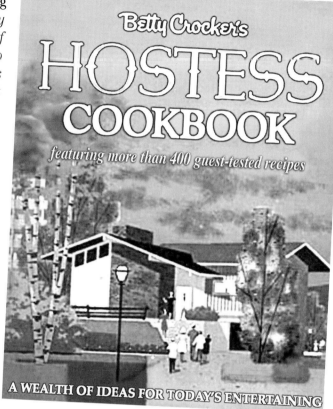

Betty Crocker's
HOSTESS COOKBOOK
featuring more than 400 guest-tested recipes

A WEALTH OF IDEAS FOR TODAY'S ENTERTAINING

MAKE A SPLASH WITH FOREIGN-FLAIR

Americans love to learn about food from other countries, and foreign themes are very chic. A ***Better Homes and Gardens*** article says: "Parties A Go-Go! Want to entertain for friends planning far-flung trips? Or give your gourmet club a special treat? Then try tables with a foreign flair. Pick the country and have a party!"

I can Flambé!

No restaurant is deemed fancy unless it flambés something! The owner of the PUMP ROOM in Chicago is quoted as saying, "We serve almost anything flambé in that room. It doesn't hurt the food much."

The famous Terlingua, Texas two-man chili cook-off takes place between Texas' chili champ Homer "Wick" Fowler and New York author H. Allen Smith. Plans for the cook-off begin when Smith writes a story for *Holiday* magazine called "Nobody Knows More about Chili Than I Do." Smith crows, ***"no living man, I repeat, can put together a pot of chili as ambrosia, as delicately and zestfully flavorful, as the chili I make."***

Unfortunately, the competition ends in a tie, when lawyer and chili-judge Dave Witts spits out his chili and insists his taste buds are "ruint," and that they will have to do the whole thing over next year!

THE Cola WARS

Unleashing The UnCola

The 7up Company goes public, and unveils the first of their Uncola commercials – a soda glass is filled with 7up and turned upside down before drinking. The campaign sends sales skyrocketing, and the Uncola will remain synonymous with 7up for years to come.

THE NEW AD THEME FOR THE PEPSI GENERATION:
"TASTE THAT BEATS THE OTHERS COLD. PEPSI POURS IT ON!"

COCA-COLA introduces their new slogan — "For The Taste You Never Get Tired Of" — and a new big bottle. Bottle caps feature big league baseball stars, and the "plaid" can is on store shelves.

DIET PEPSI follows in the footsteps of a line of diet soft drinks – first **DIET-RITE** in 1962, **TAB** in 1963, then **FRESCA** in 1966. Diet Pepsi's commercials feature the catchy girl-watching tune written by pop music writer Bob Crewe — "Music to Watch Girls By."

Diet-Rite Cola ...the one with the wonderful taste!

SUGAR FREE

diet-rite cola

LESS THAN 1 CALORIE PER BOTTLE

Real old-time cola taste _and less than 1 calorie to its name. *(That's wonderful, too.)* America's No.1 low-calorie cola.

Are health nuts really NUTS?

As the 'health food movement' surfaces, the FDA and AMA call claims that organic foods are more nutritious than non-organic counterparts "nonsense." The U.S. Dept. of Agriculture states "an ample supply of nutrients is available from food purchased in regular markets at ordinary current prices." In September, *Good Housekeeping* calls health foods "nutritional quackery."

Remember "An Apple a Day Keeps the Doctor Away?" Well, according to insult-compiler **LOUIS SAFIAN**, "An onion a day gives your diet away" and, more to the point, "An onion a day keeps everybody away!"

DIET CRAZE

Dr. Irwin Stillman publishes the *Quick Weight Loss Diet*, describing how he overcame middle age obesity and a heart attack by cutting carbs and drinking a lot of water. His diet, which encourages a strict intake of meat, eggs and cheese, leaves some participants in ketosis with bad breath and constipation.

THE LOW-CARB CRAZE gets a boost when Walter Cronkite reports on "The Drinking Man's Diet" on the evening news. It is no surprise that *The Drinking Man's Diet Cookbook* quickly follows!

IRRADIATE WHEAT ERADICATE INSECTS

The U.S. Department of Agriculture begins a test project to kill insects by subjecting wheat to radiation.

1967 ADVERTISEMENT

Are you a nut nut?

A nut nut is a person who is nuts about the fun of eating nuts.
A prime favorite of the true nut nut is the fresh-roasted U. S. Grade No. 1 peanut.
Truly a nut nut's nut.
In all the world, only two things taste exactly like fancy, fresh-roasted No. 1 peanuts.

Peanuts themselves and Skippy Peanut Butter. You see, Skippy is peanuts—peanuts in their most spreadable, edible form. And it's made in a secret, patented way that keeps every peerless, priceless particle of that true, exact, fresh-

roasted peanut taste. None of it gets away. So, if you're a nut nut—in other words, **if you like peanuts — you'll like Skippy.** Skippy Peanut Butter (The one nut nuts are nuts about.)

$1.50 birthday gift with this bucket

What's the Occasion? We're celebrating our 15th birthday. And this gives us a perfect excuse to extend a special invitation to you...because you made us what we are. Chicken Delight has grown a lot in 15 years...almost 800 stores coast-to-coast. Now, we would like to show our appreciation. ℣ Just clip out the coupon. Your Birthday Gift Certificate, worth $1.50 in Chicken Delight products, will be presented to you by any participating Chicken Delight store on the purchase of a Bucket O' Chicken (16 pieces or more) at our regular price. Gift Certificate is good for future redemption. ℣ Chicken Delight serves only PRIME PIECES of golden brown chicken; we guarantee you will never get necks or backs. **FREE DELIVERY**, of course.

A Subsidiary of Consolidated Foods Corporation. Other fine trademarks include: Booth—Sara Lee—Oxeno—Shasta—Union Sugar—Monarch—Popsicle—Fudgsicle

Almost 800 Chicken Delight Stores are locally-owned and operated. Invest $10,000 and join our prosperous family. Write Chicken Delight, Inc., Dept. K-3 Chicken Delight Bldg., Rock Island, Ill. 61202

Major Matt Mason

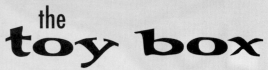

MATTEL TOYS 1967
MATTEL INC TOYMAKERS

the toy box

Revell MODEL RACER '65 STING RAY 1/32 SCALE
SP-510X MOTOR

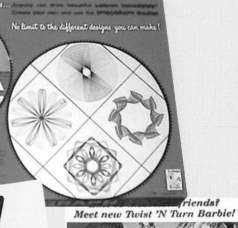

DISNEYLAND "IT'S A SMALL WORLD" GAME

Ages 5 to 10
2 to 4 players

A simple and fascinating way to DRAW a million marvelous patterns
Kenner's NEW SPIROGRAPH
For all ages...
No limit to the different designs you can make!

the AMAZING SPIDER-MAN GAME
WOK!
K-K!
with "MARVEL SUPER-HEROES"
SPIDER-MAN

G.I. JOE '67
...HE TALKS!

friends?
Meet new Twist 'N Turn Barbie!

SLAP TRAP GAME
REAL SLAM BANG ACTION FOR EVERYONE

IDEAL SLAP TRAP
SLAM BANG ACTION
FOR EVERYONE
GAME

HOT WHEELS

G.I. JOE
USMC

ARRID offers its anti-perspirant in a spray for the first time.

Colgate launches **Ultrabrite** toothpaste.

The *Sears* **Die-Hard** car battery is introduced.

Jesse White makes his first commercial appearance as the Maytag repairman—"the loneliest man in town."

SONY's first computer-related product is the SOBAX ICC-500, a desktop calculator.

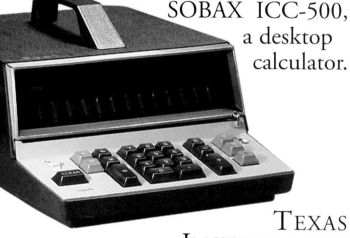

American Greetings introduces their *Holly Hobbie* character on greeting cards. She soon becomes one of the most sought-after licensed characters in the world.

BORN IN 1967 ★ JONATHAN IVE whose design work includes Apple's iMac and iPod.

TEXAS INSTRUMENTS invents the first electronic hand-held calculator.

IBM announces new features for its desk-sized computer, the 1130 system. It can now read information from five magnetic disks concurrently, allowing four additional disks to be added. Each disk stores up to one million characters of information.

AMPEX introduces the HS-100 color video magnetic disc recorder. Useful for rapid playback in normal, slow, or stop action, it is first utilized in sporting event broadcasts, launching the era of instant replay on television.

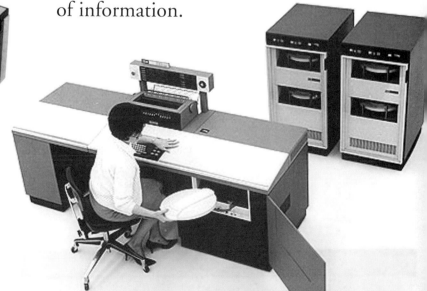

COMPUTERS

THE TURING AWARD, given annually by the Association for Computing Machinery, goes to British Professor **MAURICE WILKES** (I), best known as the builder and designer of the EDSAC, the first computer with an internally stored program. He is also co-author of *Preparation of Programs for Electronic Digital Computers*, in which program libraries are effectively introduced.

Development of the computer programming language **PASCAL** gets underway.

The **LOGO** programming language, later known as "turtle graphics" is developed and becomes useful in teaching computers to children.

ISACA (INFORMATION SYSTEM AUDIT AND CONTROL ASSOCIATION) is founded, and serves as global organization for information governance, control, security, and audit professionals.

IBM introduces an 8-inch floppy disk, the first convenient powerful data storage medium. Capacity: around 240KB.

The first issue of *Computerworld* is published.

The book **HOW TO BUILD A WORKING DIGITAL COMPUTER** by Edward Alcosser, James P. Phillips and Allen M. Wolk guides the reader in the construction of a simple "paperclip computer" utilizing household items, with a tin can for drum memory.

The Finnish telecommunications company NOKIA is formed.

Plymouth is out to win you over this year

–with a brand new Sports Barracuda!!!

The '67 Barracuda is also available in Hardtop and Convertible models.

So you've always wanted a European GT. On a small car budget.

You've wanted a sports car. Quick. The tight feel of the wheel on a hard curve. The positive grip of the tires on the road.

You've wanted a car that looked as good as it drove. A car that attracts people. To run their hands over it. To peer inside.

And you've never been able to afford your kind of car.

Sports Barracuda changes that.

It's European as the Monte Carlo Rally and priced as American as Saturday afternoon football.

We won't talk the nuts and bolts. Not even our 383 V-8, which will be ready in plenty of time for Sebring. What counts is the way it feels. The way it makes you feel.

And another thing. You can get enough optional gear to make your 'Cuda just your style. Stormer or luxury car, Barracuda is as personal as you want to make it.

'67 Plymouth Barracuda

PLYMOUTH DIVISION | **CHRYSLER MOTORS CORPORATION**

NEW ARCHITECTURE

New York's **Madison Square Garden Sports & Entertainment Center**, to officially open in early 1968, has the city's first permanent suspension roof. You can sit in any one of its 20,000 seats and still have a perfect view of the arena's floor.

The **Kaknästornet TV Tower** in Stockholm, Sweden, designed by architect Bengt Lindroos, is completed. At 155 meters, it becomes Scandinavia's tallest structure.

- The **Marine Midland Bank Building** in Manhattan, New York is 52 stories tall, and is known for the distinctive Isamu Noguchi sculpture at the entrance. Designed by Gordon Bunshaft of Skidmore, Owings & Merrill, it features a trapezoidal floor plan and about one million square feet of office space.
- **Saint Joseph's Oratory**, a Roman Catholic basilica in Montreal, Canada is completed.
- After 78 years, Chicago's **Auditorium Theater** opens for a second time.
- Architect William Vaughan Shaw wins the Prix di Rome for his environmental design.

The American Society of Civil Engineers OUTSTANDING CIVIL ENGINEERING ACHIEVEMENT AWARD goes to the St. Louis Gateway Arch, designed by Eero Saarinen and completed in late 1965.

Habitat '67, a housing complex located in Montreal, Quebec, Canada on the Saint Lawrence River, is built as part of Expo '67. Designed by architect Moshe Safdie with interlocking modules, it aims to create affordable homes with close, private areas, each with its own garden.

Science

Living in the ATOMIC AGE

December 1967 marks the 25th anniversary of the Atomic Age and the world's first self-sustaining nuclear chain reaction.

RIGHT ANSWER, WRONG PROBLEM

Nobel Prize winner in physics **STEVEN WEINBERG** tries to come up with particle descriptions to explain the strong nuclear force that binds atoms together. "At some point in the fall of 1967," he says, "I think while driving to my office at MIT, it occurred to me that I had been applying the right ideas to the wrong problems." Weinberg discovers that his particle descriptions are correct when applied to the weak nuclear force that produces radioactivity and electromagnetism.

Henry Moore's sculpture "Nuclear Energy" is unveiled on Stagg Field at the University of Chicago.

l-r, Virgil "Gus" Grissom, Edward White, Roger Chaffee.

TRAGEDY STRIKES THE FIRST MANNED APOLLO MISSION

The charred capsule. One reporter states that the inside looks like a furnace.

Friday, January 27 — a pre-launch fire in the Command Module takes the lives of astronauts Virgil Grissom, Edward White and Roger Chaffee.

The tragedy occurs during a simulated countdown for the first flight of the Apollo program, whose goal it is to put a man on the moon by 1970. Grissom and White were veterans of spaceflight; Chaffee, a rookie. Grissom was one of the 7 original astronauts. White was America's first spacewalker. Chaffee, an experienced test pilot, was proud that his first spaceflight was to initiate the Apollo program.

SEQUENCE OF EVENTS:

- 1:00 p.m. Grissom, White and Chaffee enter the craft. Immediately after Grissom hooks up to the oxygen supply, he reports a strange odor in the spacesuit loop.

- High oxygen flow triggers master alarm.

- Faulty communications delay countdown to 5:40 p.m.

- Around 6:30 p.m. ground instruments show a surge of oxygen flow into the spacesuits.

- Four seconds later, Chaffee announces, "Fire, I smell fire."

- Two seconds later, White shouts, "Fire in the cockpit."

The intense heat, dense smoke and the unaccomplished 90-second emergency escape procedure conspires against 27 would-be rescuers.

113

Physicist and professor **John Archibald Wheeler** uses the term **'BLACK HOLE'** for the first time, referring to 'a region of space from which nothing can return.' Wheeler states that **"BLACK HOLES HAVE NO HAIR,"** meaning that black holes are characterized by three externally observable parameters: mass, electrical charge, and angular momentum, but that there are no other features that distinguish one black hole from another.

A version of the **GPS** (Global Positioning System) becomes available for commercial use with the launch of the Timation satellite.

VLADIMIR KOMAROV is the first Russian cosmonaut to die in space.

U.S. Air Force Major MICHAEL ADAMS becomes the first fatality of the X-15 rocket plane program.

LITTLE GREEN MEN?

JOCELYN BELL and **ANTONY HEWISH,** designers of a radio telescope to observe the twinkling of stars, discover an unusual signal unlike those emitted by stars, galaxies, or solar winds. They briefly entertain the possibility of an extraterrestrial signal, and jokingly call the signal LGM1 (for "little green men"). Eventually, consenus settles on neutron stars as the cause, and the signal becomes known as a pulsar. The acronym LGM becomes CP (Cambridge pulsar), and the discovery of pulsars is a first step in proving the existence of black holes.

A MAJOR WAVE OF UFO SIGHTINGS OCCURS,

estimated by Air Force officials as the 4th largest in terms of reported sightings. The episodes coincide with a full year of investigations by the University of Colorado UFO Project.

I dub thee 'dubnium'

Scientists at the Dubna Institute in Russia create element 105, called dubnium (Db).

A scientist at IBM Research, **Benoit B. Mandelbrot**, publishes a paper in *Science* introducing **FRACTAL GEOMETRY**, the concept that seemingly irregular natural shapes—the branching of trees or the rough edges of a coastline—can occur in both mathematics and nature.

Background illustrates the "Mandelbrot Set"

A NUMBER OF EARLY STUDIES NOTE THE EFFECTS OF ATMOSPHERIC CO_2 AND WARN OF AN ANTHROPOGENIC (MAN-INDUCED) "GREENHOUSE EFFECT" ON EARTH.

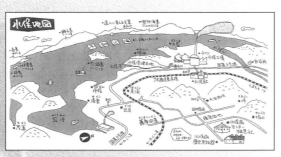

The first major marine pollution trial commences, concerning a fertilizer factory located on Minamata Bay, Kyushu, Japan which deposited an estimated 27 tons of mercury waste into the sea from 1953 to 1967, poisoning thousands of people. "Minamata Disease," which affects the central nervous system, kills forty-three in the community and causes horrific birth defects.

SCIENCE and the FEDERAL GOVERNMENT

Amidst growing concern over the harmful consequences of the inefficient use of science and technology, two committees are established to study issues relating to science and society. The Senate's Select Committee on Technology and the Human Environment is headed by **Senator Edmund S. Muskie**, and the House Subcommittee on Science Research and Development is chaired by **Representative Emilio Q. Daddario**. The main objectives: determining how the federal government can use science to solve environmental problems and to develop an early warning system to foresee undesirable technological consequences.

"It is characteristic of science that the full explanations are often seized in their essence by the percipient scientist long in advance of any possible proof."

John Desmond Bernal
The Origin of Life,
1967

Stanford biochemist **ARTHUR KORNBERG** announces that he and his coworkers have successfully synthesized DNA – the basic chemical that controls growth and heredity in living things. The DNA is biologically active, and can reproduce itself and generate new viruses. President Johnson hails them for having "unlocked a fundamental secret of life."

Ribbit, Ribbit, x2

The first cloning of a vertebrate occurs when JOHN GURDEN uses nuclear transplantation to clone a clawed frog.

CHARLES YANOFSKY AND **HIS TEAM** DEMONSTRATE THAT THE SEQUENCE OF CODONS IN A GENE DETERMINES THE SEQUENCE OF AMINO ACIDS IN A PROTEIN.

TALK ABOUT PRESERVATIVES!

Alf Erling Porsild and **Charles R. Arington** announce that they've grown arctic beans from seeds frozen since the Ice Age, setting a new record of about 10,000 years for the length of time that plant seeds can live under the right conditions.

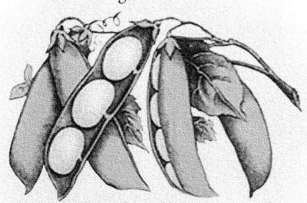

CHARLES THOMAS CASKEY, RICHARD E. MARSHALL and **MARSHALL NIRENBERG** demonstrate that the genetic code is a universal system used by all life forms, when they show that identical forms of messenger RNA are used to produce the same amino acids in bacteria, guinea pigs, and toads.

GOOD FOR BACTERIA, NOT SO GOOD FOR US...

Allan M. Campbell discovers that plasmids (which resemble chromosomes) carry genetic information among bacteria. On the negative side, plasmids transmit the ability to resist antibiotics.

DU PONT
MORE THAN POTS & PANS or NYLONS

Du Pont announces a breakthrough in the fight against influenza virus. Made from synthetic materials, SYMMETREL is the first oral antiviral medication that protects cells before the dreaded Asian flu virus can attack the system.

digging our origins

and you thought you were old!

Scientists determine that human roots date back over 20,000,000 years, not merely the 5,000,000 previously believed.

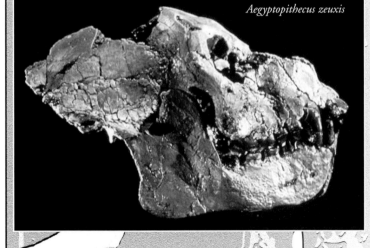

Aegyptopithecus zeuxis

IN NOVEMBER, YALE PROFESSOR ELWYN L. SIMONS announces the discovery of the partial skull of an ape that lived 28,000,000 years ago. Simons names the new find *Aegyptopithecus zeuxis*, meaning the linking Egyptian ape, and says the specimen is better preserved than other much older fossils. "As the most primitive Old World higher primate skull," he says, "this specimen tends to confirm the correctness of the association binding the higher primates of the New World with those of the Old World in the suborder Anthropoidea."

AN ELBOW BONE FOUND IN KEYNA is identified as that of a "human-like creature" which apparently lived 750,000 years earlier than the oldest known fossil of its kind.

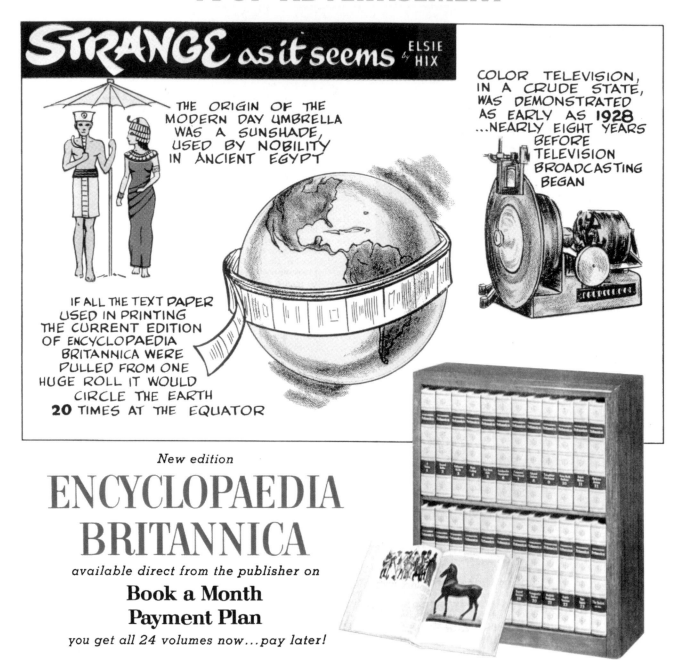

STRANGE *as it seems* ELSIE *by* HIX

THE ORIGIN OF THE MODERN DAY UMBRELLA WAS A SUNSHADE, USED BY NOBILITY IN ANCIENT EGYPT

IF ALL THE TEXT PAPER USED IN PRINTING THE CURRENT EDITION OF ENCYCLOPAEDIA BRITANNICA WERE PULLED FROM ONE HUGE ROLL IT WOULD CIRCLE THE EARTH **20** TIMES AT THE EQUATOR

COLOR TELEVISION, IN A CRUDE STATE, WAS DEMONSTRATED AS EARLY AS **1928** ...NEARLY EIGHT YEARS BEFORE TELEVISION BROADCASTING BEGAN

New edition

ENCYCLOPAEDIA BRITANNICA

available direct from the publisher on

**Book a Month
Payment Plan**

you get all 24 volumes now...pay later!

The latest edition of Britannica—the greatest treasury of knowledge ever published—is the greatest in our almost 200-year publishing history. An *enormous printing* materially reduces our costs and under a remarkable direct-from-the-publisher plan, we pass these benefits on to you. All 24 handsome volumes of this world-renowned reference library will be delivered to your home NOW *direct from the publisher*. You pay later at a cost so low it is as easy as buying a book a month!

Equivalent to a library of 1,000 books

Encyclopaedia Britannica is the most valuable gift you can give yourself and your family—the priceless gift of knowledge. Information on every subject significant to mankind is contained in its new edition. It is equivalent to a library of 1,000 books, bringing you the knowledge and authority of world-recognized leaders in every field.

Just think of a subject—and you'll find it in Encyclopaedia Britannica—whether it is infor-

mation on the rules of a sport, the background of a religion, how to build a brick arch in a fireplace, or the science of launching a guided missile.

The new Britannica almost "televises" information to you, with over 22,000 magnificent photographs, maps and drawings. In every respect, Britannica is the largest and most complete reference set published in America, containing more than 28,000 pages and over 36,000,000 words.

Symbol of a good home

Encyclopaedia Britannica cannot help but have a lasting effect on you as well as on the growth and development of your children in school and in later life. Benjamin Franklin said, "An investment in knowledge pays the best interest," and Britannica gives you the accumulated knowledge of the world in clear, easy-to-read language and superb illustrations. It is essential in every home where education is valued and respected.

Preview Booklet Offered FREE

Simply fill in and mail the attached card today,

and we will send you ... without cost or obligation ... a copy of our beautiful new booklet which contains an exciting preview of the latest edition of Encyclopaedia Britannica. Mail no money. It's yours, absolutely free! However, to avoid disappointment, please mail the attached card today before it slips your mind.

Mail the attached card now for FREE BOOKLET

Just tear out attached card, fill in and mail for your free Preview Booklet of the new edition of Encyclopaedia Britannica. Or write to Encyclopaedia Britannica, Dept. 550-V, 425 North Michigan Ave., Chicago, Illinois 60611.

118

Medicine

A news conference following the first human heart transplant.
l-r: Organ transplant pioneer David M. Hume, Christiaan
Barnard, Chief of Surgery Andrew G. Morrow.
Dr. Barnard led the team of South African surgeons.

In perhaps the most significant medical breakthrough of the decade, South African heart surgeon **DR. CHRISTIAAN BARNARD** performs the first human heart transplant.

During the nearly 9-hour operation at Cape Town's Groote Schuur Hospital on December 3, a team of 20 surgeons transplants the heart of a young woman killed in a car accident into 55-year old **Louis Washkansky**. According to Mrs. Washkansky, her husband "made up his mind in two minutes" when doctors asked if he wanted to go ahead with the operation. Unfortunately, Mr. Washkansky lives for only 18 days before dying of pneumonia. Barnard, famous for developing organ transplant procedures and inventing new heart valves, performs more successful transplants later in his career.

Louis Washkansky following heart transplant surgery.

Cleveland, Ohio surgeon **Rene Favaloro** develops the coronary bypass operation.

Reinhold and **Ruth Benesch** of Columbia University discover DPG, critical in controlling the flow of oxygen tissue from the blood; their work proves invaluable in treating vascular diseases.

Medtronic introduces two pacemakers—one external and one implantable—which sense when a patient's heart is beating on its own, providing pacing "on demand" only when necessary.

and the **Nobel Prize** goes to:

The Nobel Prize for Physiology or Medicine *is split three ways this year for "discoveries concerning the primary physiological and chemical visual processes in the eye."*

Ragnar Granit of Stockholm, Sweden is honored for "his discovery of elements in the retina possessing differential spectral sensitivities as determined by means of electrophysiological methods."

Haldan Keffer Hartline of Rockefeller University in New York for "his analysis of impulse generation in the sensory cells and the code they transmit in response to illumination of different intensity and duration, providing the basic understanding of how they evaluate the light stimulus."

George Wald of Harvard University in Cambridge, Massachusetts for his "analysis of the mechanism by which light triggers off the reaction in the sensory cells of the eye."

The Nobel Prize for Chemistry *is shared by* **George Porter** *and* **Ronald G.W. Norrish** *of Britain and* **Manfred Eigen** *of Germany "for their studies of extremely fast chemical reactions."*

The Nobel Prize for Physics *goes to American* **Hans Albrecht Bethe** *"for his contributions to the theory of nuclear reactions, especially his discoveries concerning the energy production in stars."*

Granit

Hartline

Wald

Porter

Eigen

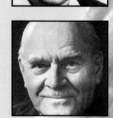

Norrish

Bethe

NOBEL

THE ALBERT LASKER AWARD FOR CLINICAL MEDICAL RESEARCH

is awarded to **ROBERT ALLAN PHILLIPS** in recognition of his contribution to the understanding of the mechanism of death in cholera, and the developing of a lifesaving treatment. Dr. Phillips can take credit for reducing the cholera death rate from over 60% in untreated cases to less than 1% in cases treated using his method.

Biochemist **Arthur Kornberg** successfully produces an active virus in the laboratory for the first time.

A major **FOOT & MOUTH DISEASE** epidemic in the U.K. causes 2,364 recorded outbreak cases and requires the slaughter of over 400,000 animals.

MARBURG HEMORRHAGIC FEVER

breaks out in Marburg and Frankfurt, Germany and Belgrade, Yugoslavia. The first cases appear in lab workers handling African green monkeys imported from Uganda, and result in 25 primary infections with 7 deaths, and 6 secondary cases.

"Our vision is a world without cancer, nothing less" is the motto of CURE CANCER AUSTRALIA, an independent, community supported foundation which funds cancer and leukemia research.

MAMMOGRAPHY, a low-dose X-ray of the breast for detecting breast cancer, is introduced.

When **DR. JANE WRIGHT** becomes Professor of Surgery, Head of the Cancer Chemotherapy Department, and Associate Dean at New York Medical College, she also earns the honor of being the highest-ranked African American woman at a nationally recognized medical institution.

Wright

TELEPATHY

The mother is keenly aware that this *natural* relationship of today will be challenged by the growing-up process of tomorrow. To conquer it, she knows a *conscious* effort must be made.

She must share the first arithmetic problem, the first dance step, the first beau . . . She must be her confidante, her counselor, her companion.

Within these pages she finds information and products that keep her in touch with changing attitudes . . . changing times . . . changing tastes.

She is appreciating today . . . anticipating tomorrow . . .

. . . and she reads this magazine, just as you do.

MPA **MAGAZINES/YOUR WORLD OF IDEAS AND PRODUCTS!**

on again, off again

Mark Ptashne

Harvard scientists **Walter Gilbert**, **Benno Muller-Hill** and **Mark Ptashne** identify two cell substances that turn genes on and off.

Walter Gilbert

Michael Sela of Israel's Weizmann Institute creates a variety of synthetic antigens that do not have to be attached to proteins – all previous synthetics did.

GEORGE DAVIS SNELL discovers that specific genes determine tissue compatibility.

Australian **SIR GUSTAVE JOSEPH VICTOR NOSSAL** proposes that antibodies work by detecting the size and shape of their target molecule.

A GENETIC ENGINEERING CAUTION

According to **Dr. George Wald**, Nobel Laureate in Medicine and Professor of Biology at Harvard: *"Up to now, living organisms have evolved very slowly, and new forms have had plenty of time to settle in. Now, whole proteins will be transposed overnight into wholly new associations, with consequences no one can foretell, either for the host organism, or their neighbors....going ahead in this direction may be not only unwise, but dangerous. Potentially, it could breed new animal and plant diseases, new sources of cancer, novel epidemics."*

MEDICARE enters its second year of operation, and many minority groups receive high-quality health care for the first time. Medicaid programs are established in 38 states before 1967 is over, and Congress adopts laws to establish maximum income levels.

OSTEOPATHY ACCEPTED

Doctors of Osteopathy are drafted as medical officers in the armed forces and the American Osteopathic Association (AOA) is recognized by the National Commission on Accrediting as the accrediting agency for osteopathic education. Osteopathic hospitals are approved by the National League for Nursing as clinical training facilities for an associate degree.

The Royal Society of Medicine Foundation, Inc. is formed by the Royal Society of Medicine to serve U.S. and Canadian members.

The World Health Organization (WHO) begins a worldwide campaign to eradicate smallpox. Due to massive vaccination efforts, their goal is accomplished in ten years.

The **Undersea Medical Society** is founded. Its main purpose is to provide scientific information to safeguard the health of sport, military and commercial divers and improve the scientific basis of hyperbaric oxygen therapy.

(The organization's name will change to the Undersea and Hyperbaric Medical Society, UHMS, in 1986.)

FEDERAL LEGISLATION ESTABLISHING A NATIONAL CENTER FOR DEAF-BLIND YOUTH AND ADULTS ARRIVES.

FDA COMMISSIONER CALLS FOR MORE STUDY ON MARIJUANA

DON'T DRINK AND DRIVE – OR SMOKE!

FDA Commissioner Dr. James L. Goddard equates the dangers of marijuana use with alcohol, and calls for removing the criminal penalties associated with the drug. Stating that more research is needed, Goddard says, "we don't know what the long-term effects are" and that "marijuana distorts your perception of reality, so it's dangerous if you are driving a vehicle."

Goddard

Are You RIGHT-brained or LEFT-brained?

Studies of people whose brain halves have been severed show that the two halves function independently.

News reports state that LSD, a drug that induces an altered state of consciousness, can produce breaks in chromosomes, creating the possibility of genetic abnormalities in children of the drug's users.

Investigators at Tulane Medical School report that evidence shows some schizophrenia is the result of an immune system disorder. In other psychiatric news, prevailing opinion says that many or most suicides can be prevented if the warning signs are heeded and treated with antidepressant drugs and psychiatric consultation.

CARBENICILLIN AND RIFAMPICIN JOIN THE RANKS OF POPULAR ANTIBIOTICS.

talk about a bonding experience!

Bonding is developed as a welcome alternative to filling teeth with metal.

LITTLE MONSTER

Professor **Sol Spiegelman** of the University of Illinois reports that he and his team have shaped the smallest self-duplicating entity ever, a virus he calls "little monster." However, all it can do is reproduce itself!

A 20-YEAR STUDY IN EVANSTON, ILLINOIS SHOWS THAT ADDING FLUORIDES TO THE WATER SUPPLY REDUCED DENTAL CAVITIES BY A WHOPPING 58%.

NO MORE MUMPS!

Kids and parents alike cheer as the first vaccine for Mumps hits the medical market.

time will tell...

As antibiotics and mass vaccination become available, it appears that in the battle between science and infectious diseases, science has finally won. In 1967, the U.S. Surgeon General introduces his annual report with the following statement:

"The time has come to close the book on infectious diseases."

PASSINGS

Polish biochemist **Casimir Funk**, who coined the term vitamin, dies at 83.

J. Robert Oppenheimer, physicist, dies at 63.

Geneticist **Hermann Joseph Muller**, 1946 Nobel Laureate for Physiology, dies at 77.

Hermann Joseph Muller

cho·les·ter·ol

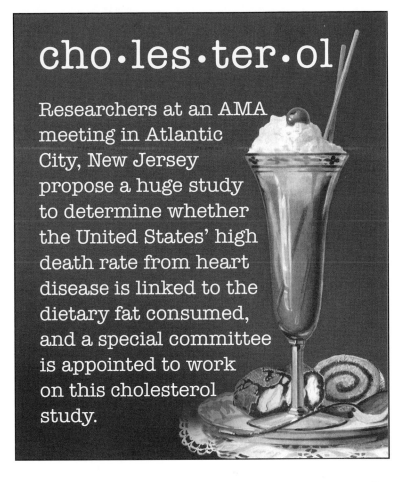

Researchers at an AMA meeting in Atlantic City, New Jersey propose a huge study to determine whether the United States' high death rate from heart disease is linked to the dietary fat consumed, and a special committee is appointed to work on this cholesterol study.

JUST SAY NO TO SMOKING

Although cancer researchers are not overly optimistic, there are advances in drug therapy, radiation and surgery. Dr. Kenneth M. Endicott, Director of the National Cancer Institute in Bethesda, Maryland says that 70 - 80% of lung cancer could be eliminated by people quitting smoking, but says he doubts this will happen.

the more, the merrier?

Clomiphene, introduced to increase fertility, also increases the odds of multiple births!

First-class travel

Exotic foods

Luxurious living

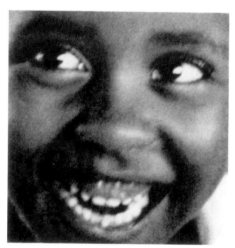

with pay

The Peace Corps isn't exactly glamorous.
You're going to be right in there with monotony,
illiteracy and an army of bloodthirsty mosquitoes.
Helping people who have <u>asked</u> for help. You're going to
work 16 hours a day and sometimes some of the people
won't even know what you're doing there in the first
place. And you will see one fraction of the results you'd
hoped for. But it's worth it when a kid in Nigeria
understands what an alphabet is and some day will be
able to use it. When a farmer in India gets chickens with
some meat on them for a change. Or when Colombian
villagers learn to work together for the first time—and
this new spirit of unity builds a health center. The
Peace Corps works in 48 countries—not changing the
world dramatically, but not leaving it the same, either.
It's tough to get into the Peace Corps. But we'll be
glad to check you out. Just write to: The Peace Corps,
Washington, D.C., 20525.

PEACE CORPS

Published as a public service in cooperation with The Advertising Council.

It's a Living

SALARIES

Johnny Carson	$ 1,000,000/year
President of the U.S.	$ 100,000
	+ $60,000 expense acct.
Vice-President	$ 43,000
	+ $10,000 expense acct.
U.S. Representative	$ 35,000
U.S. Senator	$ 30,000
Pro Baseball Player	$ 19,000
University Professor	$ 15,455
Associate Professor	$ 11,200
Manufacturing Worker	$ 5,928
Public School Teacher	$ 5,200

The federal hourly minimum wage is $ 1.40 per hour.

The Tonight Show host walks out but returns a month later when the network meets his demands for a $1 million annual salary.

Rep. J. Edward Roush, a Democrat from Indiana, says, "I believe it's obvious that one does not get rich serving in the Congress. My family and I live on my income, but there are times when it is a struggle."

The unemployment rate for all adult "breadwinners" is at a low of under 2%, but among non-whites, the rate is closer to 7 or 8%, and at 12% for unskilled 16-19 year-olds. There is a high jobless rate among unskilled workers, and shortages of many types of skilled workers.

Job opportunities for women continue to grow, reaching 37% (non-farm jobs) this year. President Lyndon B. Johnson calls "The under-utilization of American women the most tragic and the most senseless waste of this century. It is a waste we can no longer afford."

the WORK FORCE

A 20-year-old entering his first job may change employers or even his line of work six or seven times before retiring.

Secretary of Labor W. Willard Wirtz declares that "machines can now do, on the average, what a high school graduate can do."

James A. Colston, president of a New York City community college, tells students that 3/4 of them would "live to work at jobs that do not now exist."

92% of adult men have some kind of income, compared to only 64% of women.

Over half of the labor force produces services rather than goods—such as sales, banking, insurance, teaching, health care and recreation—and government is the biggest service of all. Professional and technical employment are the fastest growing blocks, about 13 percent in 1967.

The farmer's share of the consumer's food dollar drops from 40 to 38 cents, while crop production is up 6 percent from 1966—the highest in history.

18.6% of all physicians are general practitioners, but by the year 2000, this number will drop to 9.6%.

The cost of medical care rises 8%

New York passes the Public Employees Fair Employment Act, known as the Taylor Law, which says, "No public employee or employee organization shall engage in a strike, and no public employee or employee organization shall cause, instigate, encourage, or condone a strike."

The Age Discrimination in Employment Act of 1967 (ADEA) protects certain applicants and employees 40 years of age and older from discrimination on the basis of age in hiring, promotion, discharge, compensation, or terms, conditions or privileges of employment.

The 49-day strike at Ford Motor Company is settled in October, calling for wage and fringe benefit increases over the following 3 years.

Groceries

Bacon (lb.)	$ .90
Bread, loaf	.22
Butter (lb.)	.80
Coffee (lb.)	.90
Eggs (dz.)	.49
Flour (lb.)	.58
Hershey chocolate bar	.05
Milk (gal.)	1.15
Oranges (doz.)	.82
Pepsi-cola (6-pack)	.59
Steak (lb.)	1.15
First-class stamp	.05
Gas (gal.)	.28

The Price That Was

Wearables

Jersey knit dress	$ 4.95
Simplicity pattern	.60
Men's dress shoes	28.50
Jockey t-shirt	1.50
Men's Arrow dress shirt	9.00
Cover Girl lipstick	1.10
Timex electric watch—mens'	39.95
Timex electric watch—ladies'	45.00

Rock concert (Jefferson Airplane)	$ 3.00 - 5.00
Broadway musical (Hello Dolly!)	4.90 - 9.90
Life magazine	.35
Playboy magazine	1.25
Polaroid color camera	50.00
Ouija board	2.19
Magic 8-Ball	1.49
Simmons queen mattress set	139.00
Packard Bell color TV/stereo	850.00
GE refrigerator	289.95
GE automatic range	250.00
7-day cruise to Bahamas (from NY)	210.00
Sears radial tires	45.00
Car - Corvair coupe	2,128.00
Car - Porsche 912	4,790.00
House	24,600.00

Aurora plastic monster model kit $ 1.00 - 1.49

Ed "Big Daddy" Roth Rat Fink t-shirt $ 1.98

Tonka toy Hi-way patrol car $ 1.79

THE U.S. ECONOMY

The Consumer Price Index shows that the cost of living is accelerating, rising 3% since 1966.

Interest rates are climbing, and skyrocketing expenses of the Vietnam War cause the largest federal budget deficit since World War II.

Federal spending:
$157.46 billion

Federal debt:
$340.4 billion

Inflation: 2.8%

Consumer Price Index: 33.4

THE HIGH PRICE OF POLITICS

Democrats and Republicans spend over $300,000 to gain one seat in the legislature—more than ever before!

Local, State and Social Security taxes rise, and many feel the economic squeeze.

When Britain devalues the pound by 14.3 percent, many fear the dollar will be next.

Foreign creditors of the United States hold more than $28,000,000,000 in claims.

Federal Reserve Board Chairman **William McChesney Martin, Jr.** warns at the end of the year: "The entire world is looking to the United States to see if it has the capability, the will, and the determination to preserve and maintain this period of prosperity."

Government expenditures rise from $154,000,000,000 in 1966 to $177,000,000,000 in 1967, with defense expenditures coming in at $13,000,000,000.

Personal expenditures total $493,000,000,000, up from $465,900,000,000 last year. Even so, personal savings rise.

The cost of education is estimated at $52,000,000,000 - an increase of $3,000,000,000 since 1966, and total enrollment in all types of schools reaches a record 57,200,000.

WALL STREET

The Dow-Jones Industrial begins at 785 and closes at 905, with an average of 879.12.

Muriel Siebert of Muriel Siebert & Co., Inc. becomes the first woman member of the NYSE (New York Stock Exchange).

Almost half of all NYSE-listed issues gain at least 50%.

HIPPIES, YIPPIES AND THE NY STOCK EXCHANGE

In August, a dozen "hippies" led by **Abbie Hoffman** disrupt trading at the New York Stock Exchange, tossing dollar bills from the gallery. After security guards escort them out, they skip in a circle on Broad Street, chanting, "Free, free." A flyer sums up the demonstrators' cause: "Some of us have worked on Wall Street and some of us have slept on Wall Street. We are a community of struggle. Some of us are rich people trying to escape our loneliness. Some of us are poor folks trying to escape the cold. Some of us are addicted to drugs and others are addicted to money."

BUSINESS

Total spending on advertising increases to $17,000,000,000 (about 4% since 1966), and the rate of a one-time color page in Look *magazine goes from $52,920 to $55,500.*

The first issue of *Rolling Stone* magazine is published in San Francisco by **Jann Wenner**. The front page features a photo of **John Lennon** from his film *How I Won the War*.

Rollin King and **Herb Kelleher** found Southwest Airlines.

WAL-MART'S 24 STORES TOTAL $12.6 MILLION IN SALES.

FRANK SINATRA sells his Reprise Records label to Warner Brothers.

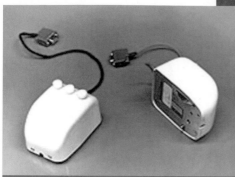

Ray Dolby

The first production prototype of a computer mouse is made by **Doug Engelbart** at Stanford Research International. It has a plastic casing on a metal base plate.

Major record labels—including Decca, RCA and MCA—sign on to use the Dolby® noise reduction system. Developed by Ray Dolby, it electronically reduces tape hiss and background noise in analog audio tape recording and playback by passing sound through an encoder, then playing it back through a decoder.

Cordless telephones enter the phone system for the first time.

There are 200 million telephones in the world and half are in the U.S.

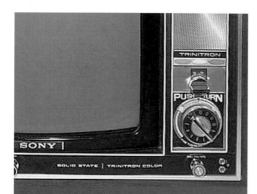

Sony debuts a new high quality cathode-ray color television tube, dubbed Trinitron®, from "trinity," meaning the union of three, and "tron" from electron tube.

Xerox's DATRIX (Direct Access to Reference Information) is the first commercial search service to search a database of over 120,000 citations.

R. Buckminster Fuller patents the octahedral truss.

The Sony DV-2400 is the world's first portable VTR (video tape recorder). It utilizes half-inch tape in a helical system.

The Carnegie Institute of Technology and the Mellon Institute of Industrial Research merge to form CARNEGIE MELLON UNIVERSITY.

New stamps issued by the United States Postal Service

Passings

Founder of Pepperidge Farm, **MARGARET FOGARTY RUDKIN** (99), began her empire by growing her own fruits and vegetables and raising livestock on her Fairfield, Connecticut farm.

Rudkin

WILLARD MONROE KIPLINGER (76), founded and edited the *Kiplinger Washington Letter* and *Changing Times*.

At his death, the publishing empire of **HENRY R. LUCE** (63) has sales totaling almost $500,000,000 and includes the magazines *Time*, *Life*, *Fortune*, and *Sports Illustrated*.

Luce

Take your pick of a Honda. The Trail 90 left. Or the Rally, one of the Honda Custom Group. These models feature a special type of tank, pipe, handlebars, seat. Ride off on your personalized Honda. Wild.

Honda shapes the world of wheels
You've got to hand it to Honda. New designs. New colors. Altogether 20 models to put a glint in your eye. That famous four-stroke engine takes everything in stride. Won five out of five '66 Grand Prix Championships, 50cc to 500cc. A world's record. With Honda, performance counts as well as style. And that tells it like it is. Any questions? See your local Honda dealer for a safety demonstration ride. **HONDA**

For a free color brochure and safety pamphlet write: American Honda Motor Co., Inc., Dept. QF, Box 50, Gardena, California 90247. ©1967, AHM.

136

Fashion

Photographer **John D. Green's** best-selling book **Birds of Britain** *is a lavish pictorial tribute to the girls who epitomize the look, fashions and attitudes of London's swinging 60s.* **Pattie Boyd,** *fashion model and wife of Beatle* **George Harrison,** *is on the cover.* **Jane Asher, Charlotte Rampling, Julie Christie, Sarah Miles, Mary Quant, Marianne Faithfull, Lulu** *and* **Cilla Black** *number among the "birds" featured inside.*

Fashion

TIME magazine lauds **RUDI GERNREICH** as the year's dominant fashion force. First making a splash with his

notorious topless bathing suit in 1964, he emerges as a designer of substance, clothing his geisha-white, heavily painted model/muse **PEGGY MOFFITT** in futuristic vinyl fashions with cutout windows. The Gernreich look is everywhere but, no slave to success, he soon sells his company in order to devote more time to designing for the dance theater.

Capezio is for West Side Story. Rudi Gernreich and Ellen Harth.
Capezio is a symbol of Chita Rivera's superb dancing in West Side Story. Capezio is part of the pure theatre of Rudi Gernreich's fashion fireworks. Capezio is Ellen Harth and every girl who will never wear just a shoe, when she can wear a Capezio.

Is Capezio for you?

When Rudi dictates cutouts...

is it chic to cut out in a Rolex? Of course. If you want to get in the swim of things like the Rolex Oyster is the one watch that makes sense. For style. For performance. With my designer favorites like this Rudi Gernreich suit. Whether you're surfing at Puerto Vallarta or Golfing at West-chester, Rolex looks right. And it's as carefully made in Geneva as most famous watches for more. Here — the Rolex Lady Datejust. Self-winding and waterproof* with an automatic date. In steel and gold or 18k gold with matching bracelet from $250. Need to know more? We have over 150 styles.

Gernreich in 1967 ads for Capezio and Rolex.

DESIGNERS MAKE

"The miniskirt is here to stay ('till Spring, anyway)"

Time magazine, December 15, 1967

MARY QUANT, who defined 60s fashion with the popular miniskirt, becomes a one-woman fashion industry, stepping up mass production of her signature designs and exporting them through her GINGER GROUP enterprise. Quant's line includes not only miniskirts and mini dresses, but accessories, colorful tights, bathing suits and a line of cosmetics.

28 year-old former Brooks Brothers salesman **RALPH LAUREN** lands a job designing neckwear for Beau Brummell. The same year, he launches his own Polo brand, featuring flashy paisley ties.

Teenage girls in the UK, eager to follow in the footsteps of top models **Twiggy**, **Jean "the Shrimp" Shrimpton** and **Penelope Tree**, turn to the pages of *Rave* and *Honey* magazines to keep up on the latest. In the U.S., *Seventeen* magazine is the pacesetter.

ean Shrimpton

"A tie was the way a man expressed himself.... a beautiful tie is an expression of quality, taste, and style." Ralph Lauren

HEIR MARK...

MARY QUANT
Wool peasant dress

The TOPS in the TRADE

- ◆ GEOFFREY BEENE
- ◆ PIERRE CARDIN
- ◆ BETSEY JOHNSON
- ◆ EMILIO PUCCI
- ◆ MARY QUANT
- ◆ PACO RABANNE
- ◆ HUBERT DE GIVENCHY
- ◆ GIORGIO ARMANI
- ◆ LAURA ASHLEY
- ◆ CALVIN KLEIN
- ◆ KARL LAGERFELD
- ◆ OSCAR DE LA RENTA
- ◆ BILL BLASS

French couturier **PIERRE CARDIN** introduces his new model, Anak, to show off his latest line.

New **BILL BLASS** designs for Vogue Patterns offer a softer, more sophisticated take on the geometric look.

Cardin's above-the-knee dress with geometric cutouts and wide belts are topped by helmet-like space-age hats.

FLORENCE
RETURNS TO THE FASHION

Knits, wooly tights and tunic outfits for off-season skiers, wild abstract patterns and riotous color schemes, all make their mark on the runways in Florence.

Jacques Esterel's "Rhapsody in Black" features black boots with Gaucho-style pants and hat.

ITALY
SPOTLIGHT

An evening dress with fitted bodice in barber pole stripes is worn with shiny black boots.

Esterel unwraps a black evening jumpsuit which reveals lots of back.

A black and white outfit with Argentinean influence features a cage purse to hold a bird!

TOP FRENCH COUTURIERS SHOW

JACQUES HEIM

CHRISTIAN DIOR

JACQUES HEIM shows off his two-piece gabardine suit with oversized pockets and a half-belt in the back.

DIOR brings this dress and coat combination for the summer exhibition. It is made of heavy sacking material trimmed with leather. Accessories include a safari-style felt hat with leather chin strap.

THEIR NEW SUMMER WEARS

ALSO CREATING A SUMMER SPLASH: A big fluffy white organdy dress with bouffant sleeves and an Arabic-style trouser evening dress.

PIERRE CARDIN

CARDIN's long evening beach dress is topped off by a big straw hat.

WEST GERMANY LOOKS FORWARD

At a German Planetarium, designers trot out futuristic space-age dresses suitable for any well-dressed lady in the year 2000. The geometric designs are all made with plastic and metallic materials.

This Year's Legs are seen in Ultrason Stockings by Berkshire

What else! These are the stockings that say "today". The loving fit. The delicious matte look, soft and gleamless as buffed powder. Delight in the space age luxury of Ultrasons by Berkshire.

BERKSHIRE INTERNATIONAL

space suit courtesy of: ACEL NAVAL AIR ENGINEERING CENTER, PHILA., PA.

A SHINING FUTURE

One designer's take on the look of the future, left, utilizes metals, plastic and stretchy fabrics.

Andre Courreges' shiny embroidered dress, below, is topped with a short metallic jacket.

Super-Royal Lipsticks

*The world's most beautiful women wear them
...there must be a reason.
In lavish new cases...luscious new colors.*

Germaine Monteil

COVER GIRL

MEDICATED MAKE-UP BY NOXZEMA

THE NATURAL-BEAUTY LOOK:

A COVER GIRL COMPLEXION

THE REASON

Only Cover Girl combines sheer, natural make-up with famous Noxzema medication to help skin stay fresh and flawless.

THE EXTRA

Antiseptic action fights germs on your skin and on your puff

THE RESULT

Glamour that's actually good for your skin

International Cover Girl Lois Dumas. Photographed By Georges Saad for French trend-setter, L'Art et la Mode. Lois says: "Since discovering Cover Girl, my complexion's never looked better. It's the only..."

New Cover Girl Make-up and Lipsticks
All in fashion shades
Make-up $1.30. Lipstick $1.10

Fabergé lipsticks *are* good enough to ea

These exquisite confections are not only lovely to look at, wonderful to wear, heaven to kiss — they're pure as pure can b
solicitous of your lips as Mother Love itself. The rubescent glow in the center is one-and-only *Stained Glass*. Starting wi
Grappe . . . *Porcelain Shell* . . . *Caramel* . . . *Bedtime* . . . *Marron Glacé* . . . *Rock Candy* . . . *Mondrian Coral* . . . *Mocha*
Stained Glass, Nude Pink . . . *Tigress* . . . *Mango* . . . *Lime* . . . *Chameleon* . . . *Van Gogh Sunflower* . . . *Cherry Glacé*.

These delectable *Ovalliptic Colours Extraordinaire* come in two moisture-rich formulas — shimmery satin or sheer sheen, a
they're by that tongue-in-chic artist, the one with The Knack . . .   *Fabergé*

What's in a glow?

could be love...could be
Superglow Fluid Make-Up

*The make-up that has a built-in glow from "Lumium", Monteil's patented light-reflector.
It's the lightest, brightest, liveliest make-up you can wear.*

Germaine Monteil

Peggy Moffitt

THE FACES OF '67!
MOFFITT & TWIGGY

Peggy Moffitt, Rudi Gernreich's #1 model, is the polished and tightly coiffed Avant Garde fashion icon. **Twiggy** represents the flip side, with her boyish slouch and Cockney attitude.

Twiggy

Twiggy on Shrimpton

"It's plain horrible to say I'm Jean Shrimpton's rival – [I'm] her successor."
Life, February 1967

"Whatever happened to Jean Shrimpton?"
Life, April 1967

Model Jean Shrimpton

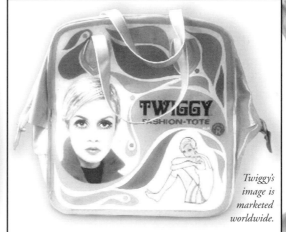

Twiggy's image is marketed worldwide.

Mr. Blackwell's 10 Worst Dressed Women of the Year

1. Barbra Streisand
2. Julie Christie ("Daisy Mae lost in Piccadilly Circus.")
3. Jayne Meadows
4. Elizabeth Taylor
5. Julie Andrews ("A rejected cover girl for a Dickens novel.")
6. Carol Channing
7. Raquel Welch
8. Ann-Margret ("A Hell's Angels escapee")
9. Jane Fonda
10. Vanessa Redgrave

Julie Christie

Ann-Margret

HAIR

LEONARD, a London coiffeur who got his start as a hairstylist with Vidal Sassoon, is the man behind the Twiggy cut. The new short, pert Sassoon-Leonard-Twiggy styles soon crown the heads of the famous and the not-so-famous everywhere.

Mia Farrow

Vidal Sassoon

Tecnique
COLOR-TONE

For prettier hair without color change... Tecnique, the one and only Color Conditioner!

Top, A Pierre Cardin runway model sports the short cut, as does Liza Minnelli,*center*, and Barbie.

1967 ADVERTISEMENT

ACCESSORIZE!

Fashion-conscious heads are topped by space helmets, fisherman caps, coolie inspirations, and scrunchy scarves. Earrings are large with serious geometric designs or playfully multi-colored and metallic. Stockings add glitter to accent disco boots, high-heels – or maybe even sneakers!

TRIFARI.

★ converse

FLEURS DE ROCAILLE

CARON
parfumeur
paris

Caron is the kind of French every woman understands.

N°5

CHANEL

She can't get you out of her mind   when Wind Song whispers your message

Let Wind Song say it for you.
It tells her you know she's someone
special. Give her the perfume
sealed in a crown.
Give it now . . . you're a Prince.
Wind Song Perfume, 5.00 to 45.00.

WIND SONG
Perfume by PRINCE MATCHABELLI

*Promise
her anything...
but give her
Arpege*

LANVIN

Vogue Patterns

AFFORDABLE FA$HION

For the fashion plate on a budget, *McCall's*, *Vogue*, and *Simplicity* offer designer sewing patterns approximating many of the outfits seen in slick magazine spreads.

Britain's BIBA boutiques offer a stylish, yet affordable fashion alternative for youthful tastes.

7080 *Simplicity*
Miss
Size 14
Bust 34
65c

8964

EASY
65c

McCall's

MENSWEAR

The fragrance for single-minded men.

'THAT MAN'

Created for Men by Revlon

Extra dry with a twist of lemon. Never sweet. Never obvious. Cologne. After-Shave and scented accessories.

WOMEN ARE DISCOVERING MEN WHO ARE DISCOVERING BOOTS

h.i.s puts you in gear.

ACME BOOTS

converse

155

WHEN YOU BUY PORTABLE TV...WHY NOT GET THE BEST

**New Zenith
Super Screen
lets you see a
wider, higher, bigger,
more rectangular
TV picture!**

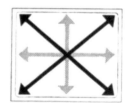

Now see a new Total TV
picture on Zenith 12″, 16″
and 19″ (measured diagonally) Super Screen Portables.
It's the total new look in portable TV. And its
cabinet is so compact, it goes anywhere . . . fits
anywhere. Inside, you get the famous Zenith
Handcrafted chassis for unrivaled dependability. See Zenith's new Super Screen TV. *Illus.*
The Shoreview, 19″ Model Y2022, at your
Zenith dealer's now.

ZENITH ®

*The quality goes in
before the name goes on*

Sports

SUPER BOWL I

19 STAIRWAY
19 **43** **118**
STAIRWAY ROW SEAT

World Championship Game

AFL-NFL
SUNDAY JANUARY 15, 1967
LOS ANGELES MEMORIAL COLISEUM
KICKOFF ONE O'CLOCK PM
Reserved Seat **$12.00**
This ticket cannot be refunded

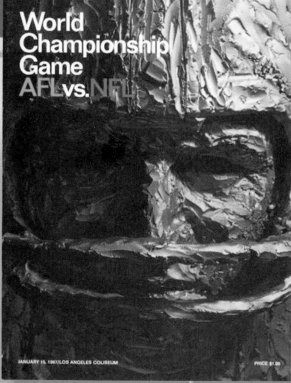

World Championship Game AFL vs. NFL

JANUARY 15, 1967/LOS ANGELES COLISEUM   PRICE $1.00

Sports

Pro football's first Super Bowl game is played in Los Angeles, California's Memorial Coliseum on January 15. Matching the National Football League's Green Bay Packers against the American Football League's Kansas City Chiefs, the historic game is notable for the play of Packer quarterback **Bart Starr**—named the game's MVP—and for the contribution of **Max McGee**, who might have warmed the Green Bay bench for the duration if not for an injury sustained by starting receiver **Boyd Dowler**. McGee spearheads the Packer victory, catching seven passes for 138 yards and delivering two touchdowns in what turns out to be the veteran's finest hour.

The long-smoldering rivalry between the AFL and the NFL flares when Packer coach **Vince Lombardi** concedes that Kansas City has a good football team, but "their team doesn't compare with the top NFL teams."

Inspired by his daughter's Super Ball toy, AFL founder **Lamar Hunt**, the owner of the Kansas City Chiefs, first coins the "Super Bowl" phrase to describe the summit event.

Max McGee

Kansas City Quarterback Len Dawson

Green Bay Quarterback Bart Starr

The first Super Bowl game pits the Green Bay Packers against the Kansas City Chiefs. 61,946 fans in attendance enjoy pre-game festivities featuring marching bands and trumpeter Al Hirt.

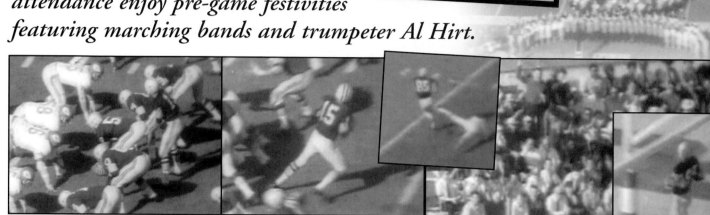

First Quarter: It's Packers' ball. After an 80-yard march downfield, quarterback **Bart Starr** (#15) connects with **Max McGee** (#85) and Green Bay is first on the scoreboard.

Kansas City answers: Quarterback **Len Dawson**'s (#16) pass to **Otis Taylor** (#89) puts them on the 6-yard line. Dawson's fake hand-off buys time for a great pass to **Curtis McClinton** (#32)— a touchdown. The score is 7-7.

Before the Half: Packer running back **Jim Taylor** (#31) sweeps left for a touchdown.

Half-time score: Packers 14, Chiefs 7

At half-time, the field is awash in balloons!

Interception!

Second Half: Under defensive pressure, Dawson rushes his pass. **Willie Wood** (#24) intercepts and scrambles to the Chief's 5-yard line—**Mike Garrett** makes the touchdown-saving tackle.

Packers cash in on the interception. **Elijah Pitts** (#22) carries for a 5-yard touchdown, boosting the Packer lead to 21-10. Starr's final touchdown pass to McGee ends the game.

Final score: Packers 35, Chiefs 10

FOOTBALL NEWS ⚫ FOOTBALL NEWS

League Expansion

The NFL expands to 16 teams, then divides for the first time into four divisions within the Eastern and Western conferences. The AFL agrees to expand, but not until the beginning of 1968.

Attendance Up at Football Games

Football attendance reaches new highs in the NFL and AFL. AFL figures go from 2,160,369 to 2,272,124, and attendance in the NFL rises to 6,160,000 — 90% of stadium capacity.

SUPER BOWL I

Television rights for the AFL-NFL championship game go to the Columbia Broadcasting System (CBS), and the National Broadcasting Company (NBC). Though the Los Angeles Memorial Coliseum falls short of a sell-out, an estimated 60 million viewers tune in on TV, and one-minute commercial spots sell for $75,000 on NBC and $85,000 on CBS.

NFL Records

NFL Championship: GREEN BAY PACKERS over the DALLAS COWBOYS, 21-17. **Jim Bakken** of the ST. LOUIS CARDINALS sets the NFL season record in scoring with 117 points, and the CLEVELAND BROWNS' **Leroy Kelley** is the leading rusher, covering over 1,205 yards. **Sonny Jurgensen** of the WASHINGTON REDSKINS is best passer, and **Charley Taylor** of the Redskins is top receiver.

AFL Records

AFL Playoff: OAKLAND RAIDERS over the HOUSTON OILERS, 40-7. **Daryle Lamonica** of the Raiders is MVP and leading passer **George Blanda** of the Raiders holds the record in scoring. **Jim Nance** of the BOSTON PATRIOTS is top rusher, and **George Sauer** of the NY JETS takes top pass receiver.

COLLEGE FOOTBALL

The **Heisman Trophy** goes to **UCLA Quarterback GARY BEBAN**

Beban's 3-year reign with the Bruins records

23 victories and 240 of 454 passes completed for 4070 yards and 35 TDs. Against crosstown rival USC, he completes 16 out of 24 passes for 301 yards.

MacARTHUR BOWL

The USC Trojans beat the UCLA Bruins, 21-20. The big play of the game is a 64-yard touchdown by Trojans' halfback **Orenthal James (O.J.) Simpson**.

SUGAR BOWL

Alabama defeats Nebraska 34-7 in the Sugar Bowl Game played in January, 1967. The Wyoming Cowboys, the only major college football team to emerge unbeaten and untied, loses to LSU 20-13 in the Sugar Bowl game played in January, 1968.

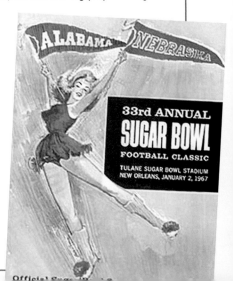

ALABAMA NEBRASKA

33rd ANNUAL SUGAR BOWL FOOTBALL CLASSIC TULANE SUGAR BOWL STADIUM NEW ORLEANS, JANUARY 2, 1967

Now that you're going to buy Color TV...
why not get the best

Chances are, this is the year you're going to buy a Color TV. How can you be sure the Color TV you buy will give your family years of trouble-free performance?

Insist on Zenith quality. Don't settle for less than Zenith Handcrafted Color TV.

Every connection in the famous Zenith Color Chassis is carefully Handcrafted for enhanced dependability and fewer service problems. There are no printed circuits, no production shortcuts.

Zenith's exclusive Super Gold Video Guide Tuner - with over a hundred corrosion-resistant 16-carat gold-filled connects - provide ultra-sensitive reception and longer TV life.

And Zenith Color cabinetry is authentically styled in exquisite period designs, crafted from fine veneers and hardwood solids, to create the enduring beauty of fine furniture.

But don't just take our word for it. Ask anyone about Zenith. You'll discover we have the reputation for making the finest Color TV you can buy. For at Zenith, the quality goes in before the name goes on.

Zenith The Handcrafted Color TV

BASEBALL—A SURE SIGN

It's Spring and the Los Angeles Dodgers arrive in Vero Beach, Florida, to begin spring training. **Jim Fareley** and **Willie Crawford** *(right)* work out pre-season kinks under the admiring glances of fans.

TOKYO GIANTS VISIT

OF SPRING!

The Tokyo Giants pay a visit for a pre-season exhibition game: Dodgers 6, Giants 2.

The **St. Louis Cardinals** (NL) beat the **Boston Red Sox** (AL) 4 games to 3 in the **WORLD SERIES**. Right-handed pitcher and MVP **Bob Gibson** leads his team to victory. Gibson pitches 3 complete games, winning all three, including a shutout.

Gibson

BASEBALL AWARDS

NATIONAL LEAGUE
MVP - **Orlando Cepeda**, St. Louis Cardinals

CY YOUNG AWARD - **Mike McCormick**, San Francisco Giants

ROOKIE OF THE YEAR - **Lee May**, Cincinnati Reds

MANAGER OF THE YEAR - **Leo Durocher**, Chicago Cubs

Durocher

AMERICAN LEAGUE
MVP - **Carl Yastrzemski**, Boston Red Sox

CY YOUNG AWARD - **Jim Lonborg**, Boston Red Sox

ROOKIE OF THE YEAR - **Rod Carew**, Minnesota Twins

MANAGER OF THE YEAR - **Dick Williams**, Boston Red Sox

COLLEGE BASEBALL
NCAA (National Collegiate Athletic Association)
Arizona State over **Houston**, 11-2.

Yastrzemski

BASKETBALL

MARCH MADNESS

UCLA Coach John Wooden

Lew Alcindor

UCLA beats **Dayton** 78-55 in the NCAA Men's Division I Basketball Championship. The 20-day tournament, known as "March Madness," takes place every spring. Featuring 65 U.S. college basketball teams, it is one of the most talked-about sporting events of the year.

Seven-foot-one, 235 pound center **Lew Alcindor** leads the UCLA Bruins to an undefeated season and the NCAA championship, and is named Player of the Year. Under the tutelage of coach **John Wooden**, UCLA wins all 26 of its regular season games, becoming the 6th major college team ever to do so.

NCAA BASKETBALL

Leading College Scorer
Jim Walker, Providence: avg. 30.4 pts./game avg.

College Coach of the Year
John Wooden, UCLA

Most Outstanding College Player
Lew Alcindor, UCLA

College coaches request two rule changes. The first outlaws the "dunk" shot, and the second eliminates excessive stalling.

PRO BASKETBALL NEWS

Wilt Chamberlain

Most Valuable Player
Wilt Chamberlain (Philadelphia 76ers)

Rookie of the Year
Dave Bing (Detroit Pistons)

Points
Rick Barry (San Francisco Warriors)
2,775 points; 35.6 avg.

Coach of the Year
Johnny Kern (Chicago Bulls)

The American Basketball Association (ABA) tips off the first season with its red, white and blue basketball.

NBA FINALS

PHILADELPHIA 76ers OVER THE **SAN FRANCISCO WARRIORS**, 4 GAMES TO 2.

All-Star Game
West over **East**, 135 - 120

EAST	WEST
BAILEY HOWELL *Boston*	**RICK BARRY** *San Francisco*
WILLIS REED *New York*	**ELGIN BAYLOR** *L.A. Lakers*
WILT CHAMBERLAIN *Philadelphia*	**NATE THURMOND** *San Francisco*
OSCAR ROBERTSON *Cincinnati*	**GUY RODGERS** *Chicago*
HAL GREER *Philadelphia*	**JERRY WEST** *L.A. Lakers*
JOHN HAVLICEK *Boston*	**DARRALL IMHOFF** *L.A. Lakers*
DON OHL *Baltimore*	**JERRY SLOAN** *Chicago*
BILL RUSSELL *Boston*	**DAVE DEBUSSCHERE** *Detroit*
CHET WALKER *Philadelphia*	**BILL BRIDGES** *St. Louis*
JERRY LUCAS *Cincinnati*	**LEN WILKENS** *St. Louis*

1966 Rookie of the Year **Rick Barry** of the San Francisco Warriors makes headlines when he signs a $500,000 three-year contract with the Oakland Oaks of the ABA in violation of his NBA contract. Warriors owner Frank Mieuli wins an injunction barring Barry from playing for the Oaks in the '67-'68 season, and sues Oaks' owner Pat Boone for $4,500,000 in damages. Barry announces he will "sit out the season rather than play any more for the Warriors."

The Boston Celtics name **Bill Russell** to succeed **Red Auerbach** as the head coach. Russell becomes the first black NBA head coach, continuing as a player while Auerbach becomes General Manager.

Wilt Chamberlain leads the Philadelphia 76ers to the National Basketball Association (NBA) Championship, ending the Boston Celtics' string of eight consecutive titles. Chamberlain also claims MVP for the second year in a row.

Uruguay hosts the Basketball World Championship, held every four years between Olympic Games. This year, the USSR wins, leaving Yugoslavia to settle for second place.

Bill Russell

Dave DeBusschere

BOXING

Muhammad Ali is in the final stages of training to defend his Heavyweight title against **Ernie Terrell**.

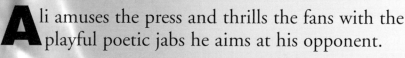

Ali amuses the press and thrills the fans with the playful poetic jabs he aims at his opponent.

*"He's goin' around claimin'
to be the real heavyweight champ.
But after I'm finished
he'll just be a tramp.*

*Now, I'm not sayin' this
just to be funny
But I'm fighting Ernie
because he needs the money!"*

Ali scores a 15-round decision over Ernie Terrell in February. A month later, he knocks out **Zora Folley** in seven rounds, scoring his 29th victory in 29 fights, 22 of them knockouts.

25c

REFEREE
MAGAZINE

VOL. 63—NO. 2 — FEBRUARY 11, 1967

World's Heavyweight Championship
CASSIUS
ERNIE

CLAY vs. TERRELL

ASTRODOME — 15 ROUNDS — HOUSTON, TEXAS

CLOSED CIRCUIT THEATER and AUDITORIUM TV

CASSIUS CLAY
(Champion)

ERNIE TERRELL
(Challenger)

Only one major boxing title changes hands when **NINO VENVENUTI** of Italy takes the world Middleweight crown from New York's **EMILE GRIFFITH**. However, this is short-lived, as Griffith regains his title later in the year.

HOCKEY

Art Ross Memorial Trophy

Stan Mikita

STAN MIKITA

Chicago Blackhawks

First awarded after the 1947-48 season, the Ross trophy is given to the leading scorer in the National Hockey League at the end of the regular season.

Hart Memorial Trophy

MVP

STAN MIKITA, Chicago

James Norris Memorial Trophy

Outstanding Defense

HARRY HOWELL, New York

Calder Memorial Trophy

Rookie of the Year

BOBBY ORR, Boston

Vezina Trophy

Outstanding Goalie

**GLENN HALL &
DENIS DeJORDY**, Chicago

Byng Memorial Trophy

Sportsmanship

STAN MIKITA,

Chicago

Smythe Trophy

MVP Stanley Cup

DAVE KEON, Toronto

Bobby Orr

STANLEY CUP

**1966-67
Toronto Maple Leafs** over **Montreal Canadiens,**
4 games to 2.

HOCKEY NEWS

In amateur hockey, Russia wins its fifth consecutive world title over Sweden in Vienna, Austria.

GOLF

British Open

Robert De Vicenzo wins the British Open in July.

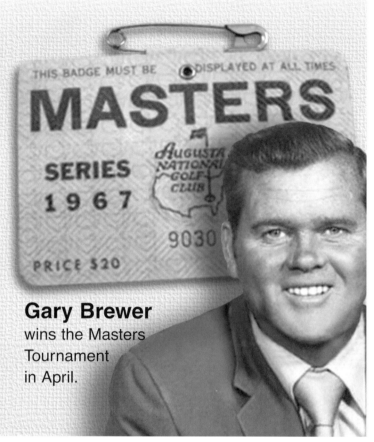

Gary Brewer wins the Masters Tournament in April.

Women's Golf

Catherine Lacoste ▶ takes the number one slot in the U.S. Women's Open.

◀ **Kathy Whitmore** wins the LPGA Championship, and is the leading money winner on the women's tour, earning $32,937.

U.S. OPEN
Jack Nicklaus takes first place in the U.S. Open in June, marking his second U.S. Open win. Nicklaus' 275 total topples the previous record set by **Ben Hogan** in 1948.

PGA
Don January wins the championship, and the leading money maker is **Jack Nicklaus** with $188,998.

RYDER CUP
United States 23, Great Britain 8.

WALKER CUP
United States 13, Great Britain and Ireland 7.

Men's Grand Slam

Australian Open -
Roy Emerson

French Open -
Roy Emerson

U.S. Open -
Fred Stolle over
John Newcombe

Women's Grand Slam

Australian Open -
Nancy Richey

French Open -
Francoise Durr
(The first native French woman to win this event since 1939.)

U.S. Open -
Billie Jean King

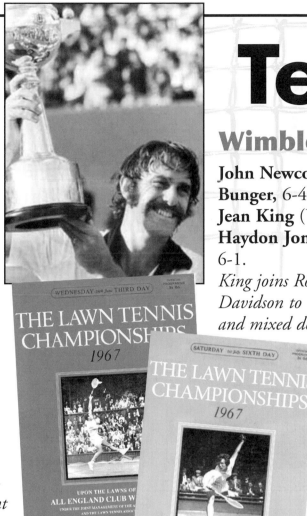

Tennis

Wimbledon

John Newcombe wins over **Wilhelm Bunger,** 6-4, 11-9, 6-4, while **Billie Jean King** (U.S.) wins over **Ann Haydon Jones** (England) 6-3, 3-6, 6-1.

King joins Rosemary Casals and Owen Davidson to win the women's doubles and mixed doubles, becoming the first American woman in 28 years to win singles, doubles and mixed doubles tennis titles in Britain.

Davis Cup

Australia wins 4-1 over Spain.

The 1967 U.S. Wightman Cup team celebrating victory with Hazel Wightman. Team members seen here (l-r): Rosie Casals, Billie Jean King, Captain Betty Pratt, Mrs. Wightman, Mary Ann Eisel, Carole Graebner, Nancy Richey.

SPORTS WORLD NEWS

FINANCIAL

New financial highs are reached in the sports industry. The pro golf tour boasts over $4,500,000 in prize money, and a total of $4,852,890,970 is wagered on horse racing. In bowling and rodeos, top pros win over $50,000 apiece.

POLITICAL

The World Weight Lifting Championships are canceled after Japan refuses to fly the East German flag or play its national anthem.

DRUG USE

The issue of drug use by athletes receives attention this year when world champion bicycle rider **Tom Simpson** (29) collapses and dies of exhaustion while competing in the Tour de France. The post-mortem finds that he had taken amphetamines and alcohol, a combination which proved fatal when coupled with the heat and uphill climb. Three months later, a world cycling record is refused recognition (by the International Cycling Union) because **Jacques Anquetil** of France would not undergo a drug test after setting the record.

ALL THE FINE ATHLETES

Carl Yastrzemski is named Sportsman of the Year by *Sports Illustrated* magazine. He also wins the year's male athlete award in the Associated Press poll, while tennis star **Billie Jean King** takes the women's honors.

WRESTLING

The U.S.S.R. leads the way in the World Freestyle Wrestling Championships in New Delhi, India, taking three gold and four silver medals.

TOMMIE SMITH of San Jose State College sets two world records in the same race – 44.5 seconds for 400 meters and 44.8 seconds for 440 yards. In November, Smith joins other prominent American Negro athletes in voting to boycott the '68 Olympics in protest of racial conditions in the United States.

USC

Four USC sprinters in the 440-yard relay (**Fred Kuller**, **Earl McCullough**, **Lennox Miller** and **O.J. Simpson**) set a new world record in the NCAA (National Collegiate Athletic Association) championships, knocking a full second off the previous record.

USC teammates **Bob Seagren** and **Paul Wilson** raise the pole vault record, with Wilson winning, clearing 17 feet, 7 3/4 inches. **Randy Matson** of Texas A & M breaks his own shot-put record, and also claims the year's longest discus throw.

Women set two world records for the mile and 1,500 meter distances. **Judy Pollock** of Australia runs 800 meters in 2 minutes, 1 second and **Anne Smith** of England becomes the mile record holder with a time of 4 minutes, 37 seconds. **Mia Gommers** of Holland runs the 1500 meter in 4 minutes, 15.6 seconds, and **Liesel Westermann** of West Germany sets a new world discus record.

QUESTION OF GENDER

At the Women's European Cup finals in Kiev, Russia, **Cwa Klobukowska** of Poland is barred because of an unspecified genetic irregularity, becoming the first person to fail a sex test. A five-step sex examination system is announced for athletes at the Mexico City Olympic Games.

TRACK & FIELD

39TH ANNUAL BIG 8 CHAMPIONSHIPS

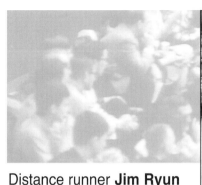

Distance runner **Jim Ryun** of Kansas University shows his stuff before his home town crowd of 10,000 fans in the mile event. Ryun has set his sights on the record. He opens up an incredible lead on the 12 laps-to-the- mile track. Ryun's winning time is 3 minutes, 58 and 8/10 seconds — a new meet record and his fastest indoor record.

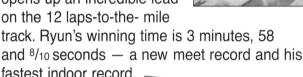

Jim Ryun sets a new world record for the 1,500 meter distance in the British Commonwealth vs. U.S. meet in Los Angeles in July, besting **Kipchoge Keino** of Kenya.

AUTO RACING

Mario Andretti's Ford

Mario Andretti

Mario Andretti wins the DAYTONA 500. The 200-lap, 500 mile race is held annually at the Daytona International Speedway in Daytona Beach, Florida. The Daytona 500 is NASCAR's most prestigious race, and boasts its largest purse.

Richard Petty takes the NASCAR CHAMPIONSHIP.

Parnelli Jones is favored to win the INDIANAPOLIS 500, but his turbine car dies with just a few laps remaining. Ultimately, **A. J. Foyt** wins the race, which takes two days to complete!

Denny Hulme of New Zealand is the FORMULA ONE (F1) WORLD CHAMPION. Hulme racks up the most points after winning both the Monaco and German Grand Prix races.

Denny Hulme

ICE SKATING

Peggy Fleming

Peggy Fleming, 18, of Colorado Springs wins the Women's World Skating Championship. **Emmerich Danzer** of Austria wins his second straight men's title, and the Pairs title is won for the fourth time in a row by Russian husband and wife team **Lyudmilla Belousova Protopopov** and **Oleg Protopopov**.

SKIING

The first World Cup tour in Alpine skiing is organized for the Downhill, Slalom, and Giant Slalom events.

The men's overall season champion is **Jean-Claude Killy** of France. Killy, a 23-year-old French customs inspector, wins 16 of 23 races.

The women's overall season champion is **Nancy Greene** of Canada.

Jean-Claude Killy

SPEED SKATING

Cees Verkerk of The Netherlands wins his 2nd men's world title with a record 178.058 points. In an upset, Holland also wins the women's world championship. **Stien Kaiser**, a 28 year-old police clerk, earns the title.

BORN in 1967

BORIS BECKER
German tennis player

BARBARA BYRNE
American rower

OLIVIER DELAITRE
French tennis player

NICK GILLINGHAM
British swimmer

PAUL INCE
English football (soccer) player

CORRIE SANDERS South African boxer

MERCENARIO
Mexican race walker

GERALD McCLELLAN
American boxer

HELEN MORGAN
British field hockey goalkeeper

JOHN PATTERSON
U.S. baseball player

KATHY RINALDI
U.S. tennis player

174

HORSERACING

DAMASCUS, son of *Sword Dancer* and *Kerala*, is 1967's Horse of the Year. Winning 12 of 16 races, he sets a one-year earnings mark of $817,941. Although *Damascus* loses the Kentucky Derby, he comes back to win the final two-thirds of the Triple Crown (Preakness and Belmont).

Damascus' only strong challenger is *Dr. Fager*. When the two horses meet for the second time in the Woodward Stakes at New York's Aqueduct track, Damascus gallops to a 10-length victory.

Damascus in the lead at Belmont with Bill Shoemaker aboard.

Winning Horses
U.S. Triple Crown Races

Kentucky Derby
PROUD CLARION

Preakness Stakes
DAMASCUS

Belmont Stakes
DAMASCUS

Winning Horses
English Triple Crown Races

Two Thousand Guineas Stakes
ROYAL PALACE

Epsom Derby
ROYAL PALACE

St. Leger Stakes
RIBOCCO

Winning Horses
U.S. Harness Racing

Cane Pace
MEADOW PAIGE

Little Brown Jug
BEST OF ALL

Messenger Stakes
ROMULUS HANOVER

Hambletonian
SPEEDY STREAK

The trotter sensation of the year is *Nevele Pride*, winning 17 races in a row and setting a new world record for the mile among juveniles with a time of 1 minute, 58 seconds.

CYCLING

TOUR de FRANCE
Roger Pingeon of France

GIRO D'ITALIA
Felice Gimondi of Italy

WORLD CYCLING CHAMPIONSHIP
Eddy Merckx of Belgium

Roger Pingeon

THE DEATH OF TOM SIMPSON ON MONT VENTOUX AT THE 1967 TOUR DE FRANCE

On July 13, one of the Tour's British cyclists, Tom Simpson, falls unconscious and dies. His death is attributed to over-exertion and heatstroke. His 1965 titles include Milan-San Remo, the Tour of Lombardy and Tour of Flanders, as well as the 1967 Paris-Nice.

PASSINGS

Donald Campbell
Boat and auto speed record holder

Primo Carnera
Heavyweight boxing champion

Charlotte Cooper
Five-time Wimbledon champion

Jimmie Foxx
Baseball Hall of Famer

Native Dancer
Thoroughbred racehorse

Tour de France Memorial to Tom Simpson

FLICKBACK has the perfect gift to bring a nostalgic smile to the lips of anyone celebrating a birthday, anniversary or reunion. Or, why not treat yourself?

Your friend or loved one will be delighted to receive the original **FLICKBACK***, the colorful DVD Gift Card full of stories and pictures from their fabulous year. The collector's DVD presents entertaining highlights featuring the people and events that made their year special. A dedication page conveys your personal message and an envelope is included for mailing.*

WHAT A YEAR IT WAS! *is a lavish, 176-page hardcover "scrapbook" packed with stories, photos and artwork detailing the movies, music, shows, sports, fashion, news, people, places and events that make a year unique and memorable. A special dedication page completes a truly personal yearbook gift which will be treasured for years to come.*

Products are available for years 1929 through 1979.

Video products are also available in VHS format.

Explore our website or call to find a **FLICKBACK** retailer near you.

www. FLICKBACK .com
(800) 541-3533